MW01039139

OUTRANK

Your Guide to Making More Online by
Showing Up Higher on Search Engines
and Outranking Your Competition

Damon Burton

About Damon Burton

Damon Burton is one of the leading authorities on SEO. His own story of building an internationally successful search engine optimization company through the very strategies that he teaches gives tremendous credibility to his methods.

Burton spent seven years as an on-air radio personality in Salt Lake City, Utah, before establishing SEO National in 2007. Damon's approach to search engine marketing works. He has optimized websites for INC5000 companies, NBA teams, and businesses featured on Shark Tank. His unique way of approaching SEO has been featured by Forbes, Entrepreneur, BuzzFeed, USA Weekly, and an endless list of podcasts and SEO-industry websites.

In addition to building an SEO empire, Burton blogs about entrepreneurship and life on DamonBurton.com. Recently, born from his radio experience, marketing, and extensive network of successful entrepreneurs, this husband and father of three also created the LearningFromOthers.com podcast. The show brings the experience of Damon and his peers to listeners across the world to help others succeed with marketing advice direct from the experts.

Copyright © 2020 Damon Burton

For permission requests, write to the address below.

Damon Burton
PO Box 160046
Clearfield, UT 84016

All rights reserved. No part of this publication may be reproduced, distributed or transmitted in any form or by any means, including photocopying, recording, or other electronic or mechanical methods, without the prior written permission of the publisher, except in the case of brief quotations embodied in reviews and certain other non-commercial uses permitted by copyright law.

While Burton has been in the world of search engine optimization for a long time, he cannot see the future and algorithms and search engine policies change. There is no guarantee that any contents of this book are in accordance with any search engine policy now or at any other time, nor is Burton affiliated with or endorsed by Google or any other search engine. Some links mentioned in the book may compensate Burton for referrals.

ISBN: 978-1-09830-207-8 (Print)
ISBN: 978-1-09830-208-5 (eBook)

Dedication

No one knows patience as much as an entrepreneur's spouse. Thank you to my wife, Aleah, for her patience and her unwavering belief in me over the years.

To my kids for always loving me. Thank you for continually reminding me to just love.

Thank you to my dad for his sacrifices.

Thanks to Joseph Hansen for contributing so much to SEO National's growth during its startup years. More importantly, for being a friend.

Thanks to Stacey Ruth for helping convert thoughts to words.

Thanks to my clients.

Thanks to my team.

Introduction

Let's be honest. A book about SEO doesn't sound like the sexiest topic.

To talk about search engine optimization you have to get a bit technical. To offer you a good balance of SEO education while being an entertaining read, I tried to seamlessly weave storytelling with teachings.

This book starts by giving you my background so you understand the experience that I bring to the table. As I explain SEO with funny, real-life stories that happened throughout my career, I then gradually transition into sharing actionable tips that you can use immediately to increase your online visibility.

Whether you are a beginner or an expert, when you read through the whole book, I am confident that you will walk away with new perspectives on how to increase your website's traffic through search engine optimization.

Here's to your continued success.

Damon Burton

Contents

Chapter One

Does Google Hate You?

You can certainly Google the definition of search engine optimization ("SEO") and get a gazillion answers that vary in complexity. For me, I define SEO as methods to improve your website structure and content so that your website ranks higher on search engines for words that you can monetize.

Search engines are an algorithm. A machine. This means that once you know how their algorithms work, you can get them to work in your favor.

If it's that simple, then why are you not at the top of Google? Because you're not feeding the machine what it wants.

What does the machine want then? We will get into that, but first I want to tell you the secret to SEO success. Yes, I know we're only on the first page of this book, but I can already tell you the two most significant secrets to conquering search engines.

1. have realistic expectations
2. be patient

SEO requires an "all or nothing" mindset. There are no shortcuts or quick fixes, no matter what you have read.

SEO is not fast

What used to take six months to rank can now easily take a year+.

SEO is not easy

What do you know that's easy that takes years to conquer?

SEO is not cheap

Considering the amount of time it takes for SEO to work, time = money.

But that's not to say that SEO has to be hard. While many people think that SEO strategies are complex, the general idea of this marketing art form is simplistic. Yet, SEO still leaves most businesses scratching their heads in confusion.

There must be a solution for "the little guy." There is. The answer is in this book, and the results that you can achieve are rather spectacular.

SEO is a science. It is real and, if you put in the time with the right strategies, it does work. My business, SEO National, is proof. Just Google us, or my name, Damon Burton.

Where the confusion in SEO exists is over how to do what and how often? An army of so-called experts has sprung up to answer the call from millions of business owners who are eager to rise above the competition. These growing businesses are desperate to rise in rank as quickly, cheaply, and easily as possible. SEO sounds like their answer.

Like most other areas of our culture, we crave instant gratification. I can only guess at the number of businesses who have paid fake SEO gurus and wasted valuable time and money on lies and half-truths. The truth is that SEO does generate massive success when you understand it and use it correctly. It is also can be damaging to your website and online reputation when you do it incorrectly. You heard me right. Doing SEO the wrong way may not only waste time and money but can have negative results and bring real damage to your company.

No business wants to be invisible online, or even beyond the first page of results on a search engine, which is essentially the same thing as invisibility. Yet, unless you have money to invest, being seen on search engines requires a tremendous amount of time, effort, and focus. This effort is minimized through a clear strategy, which I will outline for you in this book. I am pulling back the curtain to show you the same processes that I and my team have been providing to my most successful clients for over a decade.

I have optimized websites for NBA teams, companies featured on Shark Tank, international real estate agencies, and INC5000 companies. Still, as an entrepreneur to another, I understand what you are up against to get where I am. I didn't get here overnight. Almost no one does. Along the way, however, I learned everything there is to know about SEO, and I'm going to share it with you, so that you can jump ahead.

I will give you my entire process to optimize any website, including a step-by-step road map in the final chapter. If doing the work yourself isn't your thing, no worries, I'll also give you the right questions you need to ask an SEO provider to ensure their legitimacy if you'll be outsourcing your optimization.

The reason for my generosity? I like to help others. If you cannot afford to hire out effective SEO, you at least deserve to have a fighting chance against your competition to succeed on your own.

Growing a business online takes passion. If you want to grow and get ahead of your competition, you have to out-hustle them. SEO provides an opportunity to do precisely that.

Chapter Two

Where It All Began

My SEO journey and first introduction into the world of online success showed up in the form of luck. I was in the right place at the right time, with a passion that fit the trends. It never occurred to me that I could, much less actually would, make a career out of anything computer-related. Still, I couldn't stay away from computers.

I was in high school when the internet was in its infancy. School classes offered me access to computers, which my family couldn't afford, or at least current ones. As a result of their relative unattainability, I found computers to be irresistible – much like my other passion at the time – aftermarket cars. I'll explain more on how launching a car enthusiast website contributed to my career in a moment, but there it was – access to the right tools (computers) with a passion (cars).

In high school, I learned HTML. Back then, commercially available website builders didn't exist. I took that raw HTML experience with me to college. During a communications class, I was tasked to build a website with specific requirements and load it to the school server. I started to feel it would be a loss of well-spent time to build a website that would just get wiped clean off of the school server at the end of the semester. I decided that rather than let my hard work die on the college's servers, I would get my own domain and host, and grow the school project into a live website. And so, EliteRides. com, a local car enthusiast website, was born.

Elite Rides quickly took on a life all of its own. The momentum created by Elite Rides began with me creating online profiles of modified import cars. Think Fast and Furious type cars, except this was before that movie was released. Any time I would see a nice, modified car or truck, whether at a car show or driving down the road, I would ask the owner to fill out an info sheet. These car bio sheets would give me the year, make, model, and list of upgrades the car had, and I'd post that info on my website with some pictures. Little did I know that my form of entertainment would become my ticket to growing an audience that I didn't even know existed. The thousands of active members it attracted amazed me. Soon it became Utah's go-to site for the aftermarket car scene.

As Elite Rides grew in popularity, I stumbled onto a reporting tool on the server, which still exists today, called Webalizer. Although Webalizer is much less popular nowadays compared to Google Analytics, I could check site traffic – and wow! I was getting good traffic. I quickly realized that I had tapped into a car enthusiast community that hungry for what my site offered them. My natural entrepreneur instinct kicked in immediately.

Before this day, Elite Rides was built out of pure love. After this day, it adopted strategic initiatives for growth. I began educating myself on seeing how far I could take Elite Rides by optimizing it to increase traffic, and then experimenting with monetizing that traffic.

The desire to monetize my ever-increasing website traffic introduced me to Google Adsense, a Google service that allows you to embed ads on your website that automatically tailor themselves to your audience based on your website's content. At this point, I was hooked. I realized the power appealing to an audience that was hungry for content based on their unique interests.

I used the popularity of EliteRides.com to gain access to the exclusive, non-public SEMA (Specialty Equipment Market Association) Show convention. According to Wikipedia, SEMA "occupies more than one million net square feet, draws more than 3,000 media, and has a buyer attendance above 60,000. The SEMA Show now routinely brings together more than 2,300 exhibitors, occupying more than 11,000 booths." While those statistics are impressive, being in my early 20's at the time, I was there for the cars and girls.

After touring SEMA my first year, I wanted to see more. After falling in love with the event, I wanted to see pictures of past years. To my surprise, especially for as big of an event that SEMA is, there was no website with more than a dozen or so low-quality pictures. There was nothing consistent. Nothing authoritative. I immediately decided that I would build the website that I was looking for and, SEMAgallery.com was born.

SEMA Gallery would be an online picture gallery that was *THE* go-to resource for SEMA pictures. I began optimizing the website for every variation of "SEMA pictures" that I could think of.

- SEMA pictures
- SEMA pics
- SEMA photos
- SEMA gallery

Less than a year later, I was ranked #1 for all of them.

Year after year, I attended SEMA, doubling the number of pictures in the gallery each time. From a few hundred photos after the first year to several thousand pictures the next year, I continued to add thousands more each year that followed.

When SEMA held their event each November, my traffic grew like wildfire, and my pockets became fatter by the thousands of dollars earned through Google's AdSense program.

Meanwhile, I also caught the attention of SEMA's attorney, and I was served with a cease and desist. As if a letter like that wasn't enough, I looked up the attorney's credentials. After discovering he used to be an attorney for the government, I didn't press my luck, accepted the slap on the wrist, and redirected SEMAgallery.com to a sub-section of EliteRides.com so that SEMAgallery.com would effectively be no more.

However, it didn't matter. I had proof that what I knew about SEO worked, and this side hustle had a clear opportunity to be a real business of optimizing websites.

In the early 2000's, I blended my SEO experience with my interest at the time in the nightlife scene and launched my next venture, VIPnights.com.

This website acted as a nightlife portal with a directory of night clubs, their contact info, and website, as well as a national newsletter of aggregated nightlife events. Because VIP Nights was one of the first nightlife websites to offer a user-friendly, searchable catalog of clubs nationally, it attracted a lot of inbound links from other websites – a crucial factor for today's SEO. In its prime, by being a centralized listing for nightlife, VIP Nights was one of the best sources for locals deciding where to go. As a result, I became a trusted authority – another vital factor in today's SEO.

I was afforded many great experiences from running VIP Nights. Yet, there came a point where I either needed to travel a lot and hit night clubs to continue to build VIP Nights or commit to something else. I could see into the future that late nights in smokey atmospheres wasn't something that was at the top of my long-term list of priorities. Neither was traveling non-stop, knowing that my wife and I wanted to have kids in the near future.

Twenty years later, I still own the domains VIPnights.com and EliteRides. com, but they have since been archived. The content locked away for my sentimental reflection to briefly unarchive every few years.

These two project sites emphasize one of the most critical points in this entire book. The trust I was able to earn with my first two websites *cannot* be manufactured with today's search engine algorithms. It must be built, brick by SEO brick. As I built my SEO company and algorithms evolved, I quickly learned why trust and credibility worked and began repeating my success with absolute predictability – and profitability.

Fast-forward a few years, my wife, Aleah, introduced me to her favorite show, The Bachelor. This led to my next online success. Aleah loved the drama provided by the show. What I loved was the enormous opportunity of millions of viewers.

In 2007, Season 10's leading man, Andy Baldwin, and his following gave me an idea. Up until this year, when a season of The Bachelor ended, they didn't promote the next Bachelor until his season was ready to start. However, that year, they announced Andy as the next Bachelor during the finale of the season before his. Curiously, I looked up Andy Baldwin online to see what information was available about him. Surprisingly, there was very little.

That night I spent two to three hours gathering what info and pictures about him I could. I took what I had learned about cars and nightlife and jumped to create AndyBaldwin.net, a fan site dedicated to the straight-jawed US Naval Officer, ironman triathlete, humanitarian, and physician.

With my background, I optimized my site and immediately outranked the official Andy Baldwin fan site. Yes, that's right. My site outranked the official fan site of the ABC's The Bachelor, a billion-dollar broadcasting company. Next, I added Google Adsense to the site, and passive, SEMA Gallery-style revenue happened all over again. Advertisers were happy to pay to get in front of that targeted audience, regardless of which site was "official." My experiment worked so well that I did the same thing the following year, in 2008, with The Bachelor's Brad Womack.

In addition to Bachelor fan sites, SEMA, and VIP Nights, I had also made quite a name for myself designing landing pages for some of the "whales" of the affiliate marketing industry. The landing pages, banner ads, and email creatives that I developed created massively successful, high converting affiliate marketing campaigns – upwards of 15,000 conversions a day. Some of my clients' campaigns were so successful that they caught the attention of Oprah and President Obama. I had proven that I could build a website that attracted leads and then converted them to sales. The term Search Engine Optimization had only been around for a few years. I quickly learned that optimizing websites for Google ads was where the money was, and I was winning.

And then, that's when I was introduced to my first SEO client, a manufacturing company, EMS Solutions, through a friend that worked there.

Because EMS Solutions, formerly PCB Solutions, is in a blue-collar industry, they were initially hesitant about the internet as a viable channel for their marketing and visibility. Traditional, old-school, "boots on the ground" sales processes were where they felt comfortable. EMS's initial outreach to me was understandably conservative. They asked, "Can we throw a small investment into SEO to see what happens?" Despite their initially underwhelming approach, I decided to apply what I knew from my previous experimentation and success and see where the relationship would go. After all, I believed in SEO by this point.

8

EMS Solutions' results were nearly immediate. The results came so fast it was almost unbelievable. Not only did their experiment pay off, but they referred my next client: SpeedHut.

SpeedHut was another client who knew the internet "might" have potential but weren't completely sold about the viability of SEO. They wanted to know how I could ensure SEO would work? I was so confident that I offered an arrangement that I'd deliver proof before they had to deliver payment. When our agreed-upon ranking targets were hit just two months later, not only did I get paid, but I had won over another lifetime client. As of the time I'm writing this book, 13 years later, both EMS Solutions and Speedhut are still clients.

I was all in on SEO.

Of course, SEO back then was different than SEO today. At that point, it was a numbers game that emphasized *quantity* over *quality*. The company with the most strategically keyword-stuffed content and backlinks, no matter how irrelevant, won. Those days are over. But at its core, it's not thaaaat different. It's still about links and keywords, but now its *quality* over *quantity*, no matter what your cheap SEO provider overseas tells you.

If we jump in a time machine and go back to 2008, it was reasonable to be building 200-2000 backlinks per month, per SEO client. Mostly, a shotgun approach to acquiring backlinks. Automated link directories, low-quality forums, social bookmarks of any kind, etc. A decade+ later, where quality now wins over quantity, you're lucky to acquire 10-20 links a month if your goal is quality. Yet, you have to put in just as much time, if not more, as you did when quantity was the goal. These days, I would be horrified by the suggestion to build links using directories or forum signatures, as used to work well in SEO's wild wild west days.

Now, if you are looking to increase your rankings, today's search engine algorithms demand content creation, outreach, and engagement. A lot. In other words, today's SEO demands original, relevant, credible, and useful content. If you have content, it doesn't require a cult-like audience of Bachelor viewers or a love for aftermarket cars. It just involves meaningful content. Search engines are built to recognize solid content when they see it, and also when they don't.

But what is SEO, really?

At its core, SEO is a strategy designed to make you as accessible, authoritative, and relevant as possible to anyone searching for what content, product, or service that you offer. Your SEO strategy helps search engines recognize your value and connect you to the searcher. You hope the result is a match made in heaven, and the searcher turns into a sale, or, as we call it in marketing, a conversion.

SEO is a cooperative effort between you and the search engine. You drop clues – a *lot* of them – onto the internet, and a search engine picks them up, analyzes them, then does its best to match your website to a searcher's intent.

The complexity inherent in SEO arises from the sheer volume of websites, and the corresponding amount of relevant content. In 1994, there were fewer than 3,000 websites online. By 2014, there were more than 1 billion. Now, it's closer to 2 billion, and the number is continuing to accelerate.

To stay ahead of this exponential growth, you must understand how to optimize not just some of your site's content, but every nook and cranny. Additionally, you must roll out the red carpet for search engines with a clean, mobile-friendly website structure and fast page load so they can easily find and categorize your carefully crafted content.

There are hundreds of new websites every minute. Search engines don't have time to stop and figure your site out. Considering the sheer volume of sites that search engines have to explore, why would you not help a search engine as much as possible?

Where do you start?

As you prepare for your SEO journey, it is important to understand some common SEO terms, so you know where to start helping search engines out.

- **On-site Optimization.** This is the process of improving your website's structure and content. Google and other search engines crawl your website's pages to see what it's about and how authoritative it is. The information the engine finds on your website directly affects how your website will rank in relevant search queries. Create engaging content and do so within well-structured pages.

- **Backlinks.** When another website hyperlinks to your website.

- **Off-Site Optimization.** Often interchangeable with "backlinks," Off-site optimization is the process of increasing your website's external credibility. The more inbound links you have pointing to your site from credible sources (i.e., they have high rank themselves or are relevant to your industry), the better your credibility is to a search engine.

- **Link Building.** The strategic effort of acquiring backlinks.

- **Internal Linking.** When you link from one page to another within your website it makes it easier for visitors to navigate your content, shows engines page relationships, and creates a hierarchy between your pages. The fewer clicks it takes your visitors to get from one page to another on your site, the better. By seamlessly linking between relevant pages of your website, you'll minimize visitors leaving. And fewer bounces mean increased relevancy for search engines, which means better rankings.

- **Bounce Rate.** The ratio of visitors that leave your website quickly compared to those that stay. Those that leave quicker "bounce."

- **Title Tags.** The descriptive text within the top tab of your browser when you're viewing a web page. In addition to browser tabs, title tags also show up as the larger line of blue text within a search engine result.

- **Meta Descriptions.** Similar to title tags, meta descriptions show up next to a website in a search engine result. A meta description is the smaller text within a search result, and this text is used only for search engines. It does not show up in a browser tab or your website's visible content.

- **Call-to-Action (CTA).** Text, buttons, forms, or other areas of a website that are created to encourage action to be taken (i.e., to click something, to buy, to fill out a form, etc.).

- **Site Navigation.** Your website's main menu, sub-menus, and CTA.

- **Site Speed and Performance.** The time it takes your site to load, and the availability of your content is a significant factor in SEO. Search engines say to treat them like a real customer. Since real customers don't like slow pages, neither does Google.

- **Site Security.** Use modern security protocols to keep your customer data safe. This is especially important if you have an e-commerce site or one that handles sensitive information. Search engines care about this, since the searcher is their customer, too.

SEO is a puzzle to be solved. But it *is* solvable. And I'm going to hand over the missing pieces to your SEO puzzle in the next few chapters.

Every website is unique and requires careful analysis, not only of your site itself but your competitors. The great news is that right alongside the explosion of websites; there is a similar explosion of tools to help you optimize your website. I'll provide recommendations of powerful tools and software, many free, throughout this book, including a section dedicated to tools in the last chapter. While I wish I could reach through these pages and update your site for you or write your compelling content, at least I can show you where to start, what desirable content looks like, and how to find what content to mirror that is working in your industry.

According to a recent survey of small businesses performed by Higher Visibility, 54% of respondents said they don't have a budget for SEO. And 20% said they don't even have a website.

www.highervisibility.com/blog/
what-do-small-businesses-know-about-seo/

So, congratulations. Having read this far, you already understand the basics, which is more than a majority of businesses. Although I can't say how many of those two billion websites belong to the 54% of small businesses currently doing nothing about SEO, I can say that your SEO odds just improved tremendously. Let's keep the momentum going!

Chapter Three

Your Authority

For the most part, search engines aren't hiding their algorithm. And nothing is more critical to use that algorithm to your advantage than your "authority."

Sure, the super technical parts of an algorithm are complicated, but Google has a vested interest in wanting you to understand the basics.

Why?

So that you can feed better content into their machine, to better satisfy their users, to make the search engine more money. That simple realization is the key to you dominating search engine results.

Search engine rankings boil down to which website has the best product, service, or answer for what a searcher searched. Basically, who is the authority? Authority eliminates the impostors and those who try to game the system. The more you can represent your knowledge or superior product or solution, the better you are positioned.

Not terribly long ago, authority and relevance were viewed very differently by search engines than they are today. Relevance was primarily related to the number of times a keyword was used on a page ("keyword density"). Relevance was mainly a numbers game of repeating a target keyword as many times as possible on a page ("keyword stuffing"). The more frequently a word was mentioned often resulted in higher rankings.

This wild west of artificial relevance led to questionable practices like keyword stuffing white-colored text on top of a website's white background so users wouldn't see it, but search engines would. Marketers of the day also began writing absurd title tags like *"Best Keyword Keyword Keyword."* Those days are over. There's a new sheriff in town, and his name is Authority. Google and other search engines realized that relevance shouldn't be faked so easily. And authority fixed that.

Authority has become harder to achieve for corner-cutters. Although there are still those who continue to try to fake authority, search engines are getting better at seeing through their smokescreen by analyzing a website's trust, quality, and influence.

But if you feel you are lost in the back of the pack, how can you increase your authority?

While your content communicates to a search engine what industry you are in, links and mentions from other websites are what transmit authority. The more links, the better. Furthermore, not just any old link, trustworthy, relevant links from credible websites.

When you know the importance of links, it can be tempting to allow an SEO company to sell you on the idea of large numbers of sketchy links.

After all, any link is better than no link at all, right?

Wrong.

The proper way to build links is quality over quantity. If you aim for quantity over quality, you run the risk of being punished by Google in the form of being pushed so far back search results that they virtually disappear. You might experience a short term improvement, but soon enough you will lose not only your gains but be pushed even further back than before you added the links to begin with.

Search engine algorithms have been refined over the years to distinguish between trustworthy links and low-quality ones. When I take on a new client, I look at their backlink portfolio and address bad links that may have crept in through allowing uninformed staff members or past SEO providers. That way, you have a clean slate before muddying the waters with new link building efforts.

Anyone who promises you fast results by blasting backlinks is either lying or trying to game the system. Either way, you are headed down a road that will lead to disappointment, wasted investment, and potential repercussions that can take longer to repair than they took to create in the first place.

The era of SEO shortcuts is over. The age of fake SEO is gone. Real influence, real trust, and real quality is the only way to real SEO authority. And real authority takes time – time to build, to promote, and to establish the relationships needed to support your goals.

When it comes to SEO in general and authority in particular, you must have full clarity of your market niche. There is a temptation to want to be all things to all people. This mindset is so prevalent that Mark Cuban, American businessman and investor on ABC's reality show, Shark Tank, refers to it as "drowning in opportunity." The organization that tries to be too broad can't focus, and when you can't focus your content, then you certainly can't focus your SEO authority. Ultimately, if you don't know your specialty, neither will your customers.

It makes no sense to try to grow your rankings until you establish who you are. Of course, if you aren't sure who you are, there is an easy way to get clarity. Ask yourself what you enjoy selling, and then monetize that. Alternately, if you are already selling, look at what makes you the most money. It really is that simple. Follow your passion or profit margins.

One of my clients, Spoonful of Comfort, is an excellent example of following the money to a highly profitable focus, and high authority in their niche. When I was first introduced to them, they were selling chicken noodle soup as a food product. At face value, that would seem logical. However, they tried some trials with a series of landing pages that each contained a different focus and positioning based on "occasion." What they found was both surprising and sensible at the same time. They discovered there was a massive market for chicken soup being sold for emotional gifting more so than to satisfy hunger. When Spoonful of Comfort made the minor shift of packaging their soups as gifts for sympathy, illnesses, childbirth, and other life events, their sales and visibility shot up dramatically. With a simplified site design and new content focused on giving soup by the occasion, transactions rose by 534% within the first month.

This is what happens when you focus.

Your focused knowledge is your ticket to authority. The more targeted your website is, the more it resonates with your customers, and the less competitive noise you'll hear.

Your experiences in life are the foundation of your content, which can *only* be established based on what you know. You'd be surprised, however, at how many companies still believe they need to hide their most useful knowledge because of a fear that their competition will steal it out from under them. Just the opposite is true. When it comes to SEO, withholding your knowledge is a disadvantage. "Giving away the farm" is one of the quickest paths to authority.

It has become increasingly difficult to express more knowledge or clear expression of differentiation when faced with the sheer volume of competitors online. Transparency and transformation are the new currency. People no longer buy knowledge. There is too much of it readily available online, for free. They buy how you help them be more, do more, and ultimately, transform.

The smoke and mirrors approach to providing value is archaic. Today, there are so many resources online that your unique knowledge has no benefit from staying bottled up. Instead, your unique experiences are your secret weapon to standing out from the crowd.

Creating a powerful impact online starts by strategizing offline. I will use my own company as an example in upcoming pages.

The great news is that you don't need thousands and thousands of links to raise your authority. You need the right links.

For example, it is better to have five good websites linking to you then it is to have a single, low-quality website linking to you across 100 pages. The ratio of domains-to-links is vital, with unique domains being what provide the strongest ranking increases. Still, to get links from domains, you must capture their attention and interest in linking to you.

To take your online credibility to the next level, you must devote your time to identifying other credible authorities to leverage. That might include online publications, podcasts, and influencers on social media. You must actively participate in the same communities where they are participating. You must be part of their ecosystem and give value, and do it for free, before you ask for their influence.

Everybody's overwhelmingly busy. To capture their attention, you must bring real value to the table. We do this by establishing relationships, which is not as mystifying and challenging as it might sound at first. Simply liking, commenting, and engaging are accessible ways to begin a relationship.

There are some helpful tools such as PitchBox, BuzzSumo, and Ninja Outreach, to help streamline your engagement and help you identify your industry's top influencers.

www.seonational.com/ninja

If you hope to be featured or linked to by other authorities, these tools can even help you to initiate outreach using proven, customizable engagement templates. Besides the passive likes and shares online, you can also give via these email templates to provide compliments on articles written by others. By reaching out directly like this, you can share your content and ask the influencers questions like, "What do you think about this article? Would your audience be interested?" Sooner than you might expect, if your content is compelling, you will begin racking up those highly prized links. At the very least, sincere flattery builds mutually beneficial relationships.

Sharing your "secret sauce" content shouldn't be limited to PR and media channels either. My prescription for both my clients and myself is to continually be sharing core content via high profile blogging sites such as Medium, Quora, and LinkedIn. To be an authority, you must first be a part of a community. Publishing great content will not help rankings unless you promote it. The best way to promote is to build and nurture relationships with people in communities that share. Sharing creates visibility, and visibility creates an audience. As your audience grows, your influence will grow.

For example, by participating on LinkedIn, commenting, liking, sharing, you are creating a transaction of collaboration and trust. You're building up your "social currency." When you boost someone else's visibility, they are many times more likely to return the favor, follow your content, and build your audience. Then, as you give away free, relevant, and unique content, your followers engage and share, continuing to build your authority.

As you can see, you have to give and give, and then give some more. It's a lot of work. But there is no better way, and more importantly – it drives results.

Case in point, one of my newest clients found me on LinkedIn. He told me, "What drew us to you was your post about an SEO strategy you recommended that other people could use. What really made us reach out, however, was how transparent you were, and how obvious it was that you understood and knew your industry."

Better yet, as I'll explain in chapter five, I've closed approximately $150,000 this year in SEO contracts from leads that originated on LinkedIn. That's $150,000 excludes sales from other methods and was only from leads that originated directly from LinkedIn.

Your customers buy based on emotion, and your transparency and relatability build much-needed trust. There is no reason to think that hiding your unique experiences and content gains you an advantage. Your authentic, relatable content is only an advantage when people can see it like a neon sign. Be human.

One point of clarification, there is still a myth floating around that a strong social media presence has a direct impact on your SEO. While social media has its own immediate benefits, like the social proof mentioned above, it has very little direct influence on search engine optimization.

The reason social media, by itself, has little impact on SEO is that each platform is essentially just one domain. Yes, search engines can crawl these platforms and look for links and mentions, but each hyperlink is just a link from a single domain. Remember, it is the number of unique domains that count, not 5,000 mentions from Facebook only.

The idea behind social media as a ranking signal is that conversations are more numerous than static webpages and less susceptible to gaming and optimization. If large numbers of people on Facebook or Twitter link to a page, there is an assumption that that page must have authority.

Not so fast. Often viral content is low-quality cat videos. Who wants to try and outrank Grumpy Cat? I, for one, hope that never becomes the norm for authority, and so far, Google seems to agree. Also, a subtle point few novices understand is that search engines cannot access content behind gated login screens. Posts on Facebook that are set to be visible to friends only (not public) are limited to being seen by friends only. And since Google can't see that friend-only content, there is nothing it can do with it.

Don't give up altogether on social media. It has its own benefits. Just not in SEO.

I tell my clients that to have measurable SEO impact, they are better served to blog regularly. This is typically met with a great deal of anxiety since writing content is time-consuming. After all, unless you are a blogger, blogging is not your company's focus.

Still, the fact remains, the payoffs of intensive blogging are worth the investment, and writing strategies and inspiration are plentiful. Rather than abandon my clients to the overwhelming task of trying to create fresh content every week, I help them to build a 52-week content calendar, which I'll show you in chapter six, to front-load their blogging efforts, and create quality content in large batches. Working in batches like this saves an infinite amount of time.

It is precisely this volume of content that has to be created to build effective authority. When a company embraces this, hiring outside bloggers can be extremely attractive. While hiring out your blog writing is a good idea in theory, and totally doable if done correctly, I strongly advise you to have some checks and balances in place to manage your outsourced content. We are talking about your content here and your authority. Any content you push out into the web must be robust and original. If it isn't unique or relevant, you are just wasting time and money and getting nowhere.

Consider tackling your own content, at least in the beginning, so you can establish a process and find your desired tone of voice. Then you can outsource it once those processes are established. Otherwise, inaccurate content published under your name, regardless if an assistant drafted it, is a bad look on you and your company, a mistake that your competition will be waiting to capitalize on or remind you about for years to come.

Speaking of competitors, they are a source of information that would be a mistake to ignore. You not only can but should take the time to see what content your competitors are pushing out and what keywords they are focusing on. SpyFu (www.seonational.com/spy) is a free and handy tool for doing precisely that. It allows you to see what keywords your competitors are showing up for, both organic and pay per click. It is wise to evaluate your top competitors, examining how strategic they are, so you know where your best opportunities to capitalize are.

Google's Keyword Ad Planner is another free tool to help you quickly pinpoint frequent keyword searches and how competitive they are to pursue.

https://ads.google.com/aw/keywordplanner/home

Of course, the info that Google provides is frequently changing, and always delivers broad generalities. But any info is better than nothing, and this planner is a great tool to use as a loose gauge of what keywords are searched more or less than others, and which have more or less competition.

An important part of keyword analysis is to remember not to lose sight of your specific niche and your target market. The more refined your focus, the better results you will see. All it takes is one person to convert to a sale, so you are far better off finding a smaller market and addressing them directly. After all, ten sales from 100 targeted visitors are far better than one sell from 1,000 non-targeted visitors.

Authority is about consistency. It grows over time and relies on the most understated SEO metric – earning real trust and influence with real people. None of that can be forced, faked, or rushed.

Of course, you still need to build a well-designed, fast, useful website with complement your great content. By now, I am sure you understand why outsourcing your SEO to a budget provider that focuses solely on the quantity of links instead of quality, or other old-school strategies, will ultimately get you nowhere. Authenticity and relationships now drive SEO. When you do the work to provide value and build organic relationships, authority and higher SEO rankings will be your rewards.

Chapter Four

It's Alive! ... Now What?

Congratulations. You've just launched a stunning new website. You have every right to be proud of it. It is far better than anything your competition has. It's irresistible. But where are the customers? Crickets.

You built it, but no one came. Now what?

Don't panic.

This is the point when I am introduced to many clients – the moment they realize their brilliant website is invisible. They have enough of a basic understanding of SEO to recognize that it provides the solution they need. They want to pull up to the SEO drive-thru window, have someone fix their keywords and build some links for a few bucks, then drive off into the sunset. By now, like me, you know that is not going to be enough, but they are right about where to start.

Backlinks

There are few better ways to improve search engine visibility than acquiring quality backlinks. It is the lifeblood that pumps free traffic to your site from search engines. But link building absolutely must be done correctly.

Search engines "crawl" the links from one website to another, much like nerve impulses that travel through our bodies. Without nerve impulses, there is no mind-to-body action, and without backlinks, there is no connecting thread that leads search engines to your site.

Techniques for building links are diverse and vary in difficulty, as well as effectiveness. Besides being vital to SEO, link building is also one of the more challenging strategies to do effectively.

Let me save you from wasting time with a few specific types of low-quality backlinks that you should avoid pursuing. I'll be very blunt here, don't build these types of backlinks.

- Directories
- Social bookmarking sites
- Forum signatures
- Forum profiles

Period. Ever.

Here are a few examples of what some low-quality backlinks look like.

WORLD LINK DIRECTORY

WLD Directory is human edited free general web directory.Free web directory listing with review in maximum 24 hours

WLD Directory-Free web directory » The Best Memory Foam Mattress by Design

Title: » The Best Memory Foam Mattress by Design

URL: http://luxisleep.com/ ◄——— low quality link directory

Listed in the following Categories: - Business Services

Description: Luxi is the best memory foam mattress by design, Luxi's memory foam mattress is the most comfortable mattress around. Free shipping and return on all purchases.

I am starting with what *not* to do when building links since it is such a strenuous process, which can tempt even the best of us to cheat, just a little. But when it comes to SEO, as you are likely gathering by now, cheating does not pay off.

The Empty Promise of Easy Links

Directories and social bookmark sites exist almost exclusively to create low-quality catalogs of links. Most SEO companies know that, and Google *certainly* knows it. Google can quickly identify patterns and flag sites that exist solely to harbor links. If you submit your site to such low-quality links and show up next to poorly written articles about little blue pills, your site becomes guilty by association. In the world of search engines, ignorance of the rules is no excuse.

Some say, "relevant local directories that are industry-specific and have moderators quality control them are still good." There may be some truth to that statement, *maybe*, but there are no clear indicators to define relevance and quality. This leaves you wasting days upon days submitting links to hundreds of directories for the small chance of finding a potentially reasonable directory on the thousandth try. SEO is difficult enough without adding layers of this type of intensive, unpredictable effort.

I do want to be clear; there is a big difference between being listed in a major business directory (Yelp, Google My Business, Yellow Pages, Dun & Bradstreet, Manta, etc.) versus trying to raise your SEO ranking by being listed in spammy, link-only directories that you have never heard of.

As a rule of thumb, any directory that is full of ads, or that requires you to place a reciprocal link to their site on your website is likely toxic and should be avoided at all costs.

Forum Automation

Forum signatures and forum profile backlinks are also a waste of time. Like directories, Google knows that forum profiles and signatures are abused. If you can spot a pattern in how forums present links in signatures, Google certainly can, too, and anyone who recommends posting in a forum solely for signature links is out of date with their strategies. They either don't know what they are talking about, or they hope you don't.

That said, authentic, value-based posting in forums can potentially be a benefit to SEO. Increasing awareness with people in your niche can offer potential link building opportunities:

- **Identify other people with a common interest**. This is the online version of networking. When you comment, provide an opposing or supporting viewpoint, articulate your views effectively, and offer expertise, then you attract attention. This can lead to offers of visibility through other blogs, articles, or podcasts, most of which bring links pointing back to your site. You earned these links by providing valuable expertise in an online community – again, not because you had a link in your forum profile or signature.

- **Identify commonly asked questions** from people in your niche. If you have a solution, this provides the content that you can then write about on your site.

- **Identify trends** or developments in your industry. Just like the approach of answering commonly asked questions, this creates traffic, and yes, links. It really is that simple. It's just not fast, easy, or brainless, and it has nothing to do with your forum signature. It has everything to do with your content and participation and credibility within online communities.

Forums serve one important purpose: to help people find information and connect. That helps build authority, not links, per se. Therefore, forums can indirectly lead to linking opportunities by networking. They are not usually directly quality link building opportunities.

Mission Impossible: Removing Bad Backlinks

The goal in building links is to have them do the work they are meant to do - provide SEO value. But before you get too excited and start link building, it's worth spending time reviewing historical backlinks to see if there are any low-quality ones worth cleaning up. If you are like many of my clients who have been around for a minute, you likely have some bad, unnatural links pointing to your site that need to be dealt with. Especially if you have been involved in SEO link building before the previously discussed Penguin algorithm from Google.

To succeed, you must uncover bad backlinks and disarm them. I say "disarm" since, unless you own or have access to a website with the bad backlink, you can't remove it. So what do you do if you *do* have a bad back-link on a website that you don't own or have access to? You ask Google for forgiveness and "disavow" it.

Introduced in October of 2012, alongside Penguin, the disavow tool provides a way to plead your case with Google, so it overlooks detrimental links pointing to your website.

https://www.google.com/webmasters/tools/disavow-links-main

After all, Google isn't out to undercut their customer base – you, the webmaster that provides the content that search engines live or die by.

And for those that care, Bing also later came out with a disavow tool.

https://www.bing.com/webmaster/help/how-to-disavow-links-0c56a26f

This is not a tool to use lightly or randomly. Google states very clearly that "in some circumstances, incoming links can affect Google's opinion of a page or site. ... we recommend that you remove as many spammy or low-quality links from the web as possible."

https://support.google.com/webmasters/answer/2648487

Keep in mind that Google implies that they want you to do as much work as you can to remove spammy or low-quality links yourself before you disavow the remaining links.

Below is the general process, but understand that what follows is not a full disavowal how-to guide, because there is already a gazillion of those guides available:

https://www.google.com/search?q=how+to+disavow

In general, disavowing links is a four-step process.

- You'll need to identify backlinks that point to your website.
- Further, identify which of the links are spammy or low quality.
- Create a text file containing only the links that you want to distance yourself from.
- Submit to Google.

https://www.google.com/webmasters/tools/disavow-links-main

To be clear – disavowing links doesn't remove them. It only means you ask Google to disassociate your website from them.

After disavowing backlinks, what remains is a waiting game. You will need to wait until Google digests all of the information that you just sent it so that it can apply new ranking calculations based on the links you told it to ignore.

Throughout this "link detox" process, you should only be disavowing irrelevant links that you're not sure where they came from, or you know they were made to manipulate Google's results. Likewise, it is crucial that you not be careless while disavowing backlinks so you don't distance yourself from links that may have some positive value.

There are some SEO's that say disavowing links is a waste of time because Google doesn't penalize links as much these days. Instead, they say that Google tries only to reward good links instead of penalizing bad links. That may have some truth to it but, as long as Google still endorses their disavow tool, there is no good reason not to use it.

With billions of pages on the internet, it's best to gather your backlink portfolio from multiple sources and overlap the results to paint a complete picture. Here are some resources to export your backlinks from.

Free and paid resources:

- Open Link Profiler - www.seonational.com/olp
- WebMeUp - www.seonational.com/webmeup

Paid only resources:

- SEOspyglass - www.seonational.com/backlinks
- Majestic - www.seonational.com/majestic
- Ahrefs - www.seonational.com/ahrefs
- LinkResearchTools - www.seonational.com/lrt

By combining your results from multiple sources, you can get a thorough assessment of what your link situation is. Once you organize your backlink portfolio, visit each URL and consider if:

- your link is on a spammy website
- the linking website shares the same IP as other spammy websites
- there is an excessive amount of links (good indicator of low-quality)
- the website doesn't show up for its own name on Google (good indicator that it's been penalized)

Decide whether or not the link is good. If you don't trust it, submit the link to Google Search Console in a disavow file.

Press Releases

Before we talk about press releases, some other SEO's will already be saying "bah humbug." This is because they say press releases should not be used as a link building strategy. I agree.

I'm not talking about press releases for backlinks. Most press release websites add a "nofollow" status to links, which suggests to Google to not give the link value. And press release sites that don't nofollow links, Google usually knows it's a press release site and ignores the link anyway.

Instead, the value in press releases comes from potential syndication. This means that you may get picked up by industry websites. Since much of ranking highly on search engines is based on brand awareness and credibility, it is important to create a "buzz" about your product, service, or website. Sure, a backlink is of value. But when other websites mention you or your domain but don't hyperlink it, that is called a citation. And the more relevant the websites are that cite you, the more credible your website becomes.

Keep in mind that writing a press releases is different than writing for a blog. Blog content goes on your website and is about your industry. Press releases are submitted to external news websites and should be specifically about you or your business, not the industry as a whole.

Usually, I hear some grumbling at this point with questions like:

- What do I write a press release about?
- How do I structure the press release?

- Where do I submit the press release after I write one?

Glad you asked. Here are a few general topics to potentially tap into to write a press release about.

- Attendance of a conference/convention/workshop
- Financial reports or growth data
- Unveiling of a new product, service or location
- Events that your business is hosting
- Expansions or upgrades to your equipment or facilities
- Awards that you have received (or given to others)
- Joint ventures
- Preventions that your service helps with (illness, disaster)
- Media coverage your company was featured within
- New management/staff additions/promotions
- Case study results

Now you have your idea of what to write about. How do you start writing it? Here is a common outline that should be accepted by just about any news or press outlet.

- **First Paragraph:** Use the first paragraph of your press release to summarize the news that you are sharing in the press release. Start with an introduction of who you or your company are. Why you are an authority on the topic being discussed, and maybe include a statistic for credibility, if available, about the topic.
- **Second Paragraph:** The second paragraph is an excellent opportunity to validate the topic and you being an authority on the subject by providing a quote, or a testimonial.
- **Third Paragraph:** The third paragraph is where you can dive into details about the topic at hand. To support your statements about the topic, you can also add data, facts, references, credibility, etc. Social proof is also good reinforcement. Talk about how many

people are involved, benefit from the topic, or recognizable people that use your product.

- **Fourth Paragraph:** Quotes and testimonials add power to a press release. Add a quote or testimonial here.

- **Final Paragraph:** Summarize everything that has been discussed in the previous paragraphs and wrap up with some information about you or your company again. Include a call-to-action or a way for readers to contact you for more information about you, your company, or the press release's topic.

You have your topic locked in and press release draft completed. What now? Where do you submit the press release after you write one? Let's start with where you should *not* submit it. Never submit your news to a free press release site, unless you want to look bad showing up next poorly written announcements about knockoff Gucci bags or that same tiny blue pill for men.

Press Release - Online Pharmacy offer Generic Viagra at Discount Price

By offering Generic Viagra at reasonable prices without compromising on the quality, Samrx.com has played a key role in resurgence of this medication. This website also offers high protection to the customers when it comes to their credit card payments and personal information. It has got huge customer base in the western countries due to efficient medications and trustworthiness. When it comes to bulk purchases, the prices offered on this website are cheaper when compared to market rates.

Using a paid website is an easy way to eliminate most possibilities of being guilty by association from showing up next to someone else's low-quality announcement. Why? Because most poor-performing SEO's aim for high-quantity, automated tactics instead of higher quality results, and throwing in a payment requirement inhibits automated solutions.

The next consideration to gauge which outlets you can submit a press release to is if they distribute submitted content to Google News. If the outlet can syndicate to Google News, then they are required to follow specific quality control guidelines. Those guidelines mean that they will require you and all the other people submitting to them to follow those guidelines as well.

Here is one of my favorite press release distribution services to recommend.

www.seonational.com/press

If your goal is simply to get into Google News, this news distribution network offers options that start at less than $100. If you have broader distribution needs and want to get in front of the Associated Press and thousands of journalists, they have additional options for not too much more.

While the main goal is to increase your credibility in the eyes of search engines, the immediate traffic boost that's seen in the screenshot below comes one day after submitting a press release to this network and is icing on the cake.

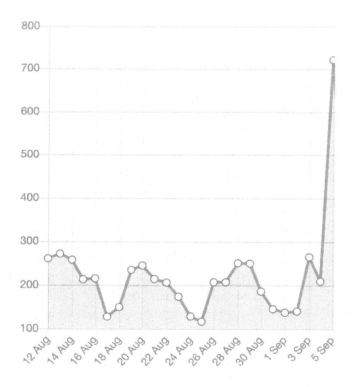

Want more options? Here are two other affordable press release websites:

- www.seonational.com/pru
- www.seonational.com/kisspr

When I share these options in presentations, I am often asked why the widely known website PRweb.com is not on the list. While PRweb is certainly an option, it doesn't make sense if your goal is simply to be syndicated in Google News. The other options above do the same thing, but for cheaper. Now, if you have a legit announcement beyond the scope of a press release just for SEO purposes, and are willing to pay a few hundred dollars, then you can throw PRweb back in the mix.

Another common question I get about submitting press releases is if it is worth paying an up-charge for a backlink in your announcement? No. Here's why.

- The sites above allow backlinks at no additional cost.
- Most links in press releases are nofollowed anyway.

Link Building Secrets

Although the best link building strategies involve time-intensive content and outreach efforts, for less competitive industries, you might be able to get away with a few "gray hat" or "old school" tactics.

Do tell?

Some people still find success with guest posting and, for less competitive industries, even blog commenting.

- Guest posting is the process of writing valuable content for other websites to publish as their own in return for the ability to include a backlink of your choice within the content.
- Blog commenting is the process of finding relevant posts, reading them, and contributing a valuable reply to the conversation.

If you engage in blog commenting, I strongly recommend that you do it manually and not automated. While manually building links means it takes more time, there are ways to help speed up the process of looking for backlink opportunities while maintaining quality control and peace of mind where you submit to.

One free tool is called DropMyLink.com. This website helps you find websites in your target industry based on keywords and website patterns, speeding up the time you spend looking for link building opportunities to then manually submit to.

After you find a potential website to submit your link to, I recommend that you manually review that site for the following.

- Review its content for relevancy before submitting your comment.
- Make sure that comments already submitted by other people have been screened and moderated and don't look spammy. The last thing that you want to do is submit your comment next to a wall of unmoderated, spammy links and end up being spammy by association.
- Check the website for excessive ads. If everywhere you look is ad after ad after ad, Google will devalue the website, lessening the benefits of you spending time submitting to it.

As you manually review these websites using the above criteria, you will quickly see that had you automated this process without your human eye, there are a lot places your backlink may have ended up that you would have regretted later.

Another link building strategy that I enjoy is crowd-sourcing replies from industry experts ("roundup articles"). You feature their comments, notify them that their contribution is live, and hope they are excited enough to share their feature and link back to you. Here is an example where I was featured on someone else's website in one of their roundup articles.

Top 29 Website Design Ideas & Resources

By Anna Dizon on March 20, 2018 | Create a Website, Marketing, Online Marketing | Comments (4)

Great website designs combine functionality with aesthetics, meaning your website should not only look good, it should also effectively convert traffic to sales.

We put together this list of the top 29 website design ideas and resources for all those looking to get the most out of their website design in 2018. We have expert tips, followed by web resources which can improve your website design.

Here are the top 29 website design ideas and resources:

3. Embrace Minimalism

Damon Burton, President, SEO National

If you are launching a website, you want to make sure it will be useful, understandable, unobtrusive, and aesthetically pleasing. One style gaining traction in web design is minimalism, which embraces the use of negative space to emphasize a design's effectiveness. Simplifying designs and eliminating clutter can be advantageous...

One more link building tactic that I'm a fan of is using public data to make informative graphics or shareable assets. Here is an infographic that I made using public data about states that have the highest and lowest percentages of income tax that we used for a client that specializes in job placement, recruiting, and staffing.

By creating valuable assets that people in your target audience are likely to enjoy or benefit from then those same people are also likely to share those assets, attracting backlinks.

If you make a really compelling piece of content, you may get lucky and go viral. Elli Bishop at Clearlink provides an example with her team's genius "The Marvel Movie Marathon Dream Job" campaign.

https://www.cabletv.com/blog/marvel-movie-marathon-dream-job

Clearlink came up with a link building campaign to attract backlinks for their website, CableTV.com, that collected and sold leads to cable television providers like Comcast, Dish Network, etc. The idea was to award one lucky Marvel lover $1,000 for watching around 40 hours of Marvel movies, all while live-tweeting throughout their binge session. Once their campaign was ready, they started reaching out to notify various media outlets. It eventually went viral. The results? Elli reported that the campaign led to acquiring backlinks from news outlets like ABC and Forbes, and generated $500,000+ in publicity.

https://www.slideshare.net/elli1186/outreach-from-scratch-how-
to-hire-the-right-people-to-earn-the-coverage-you-need

If you're not sure where to start reaching out, consider hitting up influencers and rockstars in your industry. They already have a large audience, are
actively sharing other people's content, and can rapidly drive traffic to your
content. One backlink from them can be more valuable than hundreds of
low-quality links.

There are excellent tools to help you get a head start on identifying influencers and websites relevant to your industry, including the contact information of the people behind those websites. One such tool that is an industry
favorite is BuzzSumo.

www.seonational.com/buzz

With BuzzSumo, you can also research what content is performing well
on other websites and on social media, including what domains share that
content. BuzzSumo even lets you test-drive their software for free.

How Many Links Will It Take?

Once you grasp the importance of links and the necessity of quality over
quantity, the next question usually asks how many links will it take to rank
number one? The easy answer, and the one most SEO providers give, is
probably the answer that you don't want to hear. "It depends."

This response is not intentionally vague but is the unfortunate truth.

- It depends on your industry.
- It depends on how many links your competitors have.
- It depends on the quality of links that your competitors have.

For example, a single, high-quality link from a high-quality website like
The Wall Street Journal or Associated Press could be worth hundreds, even
thousands of links from otherwise low-quality websites. Therefore, trying to

accelerate your link building process through automated backlink programs is a doomed endeavor.

There are no shortcuts available with backlinks anymore. Ever since Google's Penguin algorithm came out in 2012, the entire process of link building has shifted from a quantity approach to quality.

https://en.wikipedia.org/wiki/Google_Penguin

Depending on how many bad links you have, Google's Penguin algorithm may devalue your SEO efforts or, worse, penalize your website never to be seen again until you deal with these skeletons in your closet.

> Cringey industry joke:
>
> Where is the best place to hide a dead body?
> On the second page of Google.
>
> *(because nobody ever goes past page one)*

The days of buying, trading, and building just plain irrelevant backlinks are long gone. Google makes no secret that they are getting even more granular and discounting or ignore links that shouldn't have value.

With all of this in mind, if you want to get a rough idea of the number of backlinks you'll need to have a fighting chance, check out the Keyword Explorer tool from Ahrefs.

www.seonational.com/ahrefs

By entering a keyword that you want to rank for, you can get an idea of how many links your competitors have that rank in the position that you want. There are tons of other pieces of information provided as well, such as how many sites compete with you for that target keyword, and an estimate for how much traffic that keyword gets.

Let's check out an example. Here are what the results look like for the phrase "healthy juices" using the Ahrefs tool.

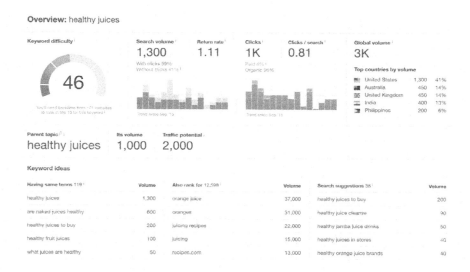

If you look at the top left of the Ahrefs image, you will see a "keyword difficulty" score of 46, and under that, in the small print, it suggests that in order to rank tenth on Google, you will need 71 backlinks for that particular search. That is Ahrefs opinion of how many links you will need – more or less. Now, building the right ones is the real work.

While Ahrefs is an industry favorite, it is a paid service. If you're looking for a free option, Open Link Profiler is worth checking out.

www.seonational.com/olp

Open Link Profiler won't give you as many insights and data points as Ahrefs, but it will tell you an estimate of how many backlinks your competitors have.

Before Penguin, it wasn't uncommon for SEO companies to build thousands of links per month, per client. Now that the process is more of a manual approach, it still takes the same amount of time to acquire just 10 - 20 links per month, per client.

But that's not a setback – it is just a new process. In some ways, it is an advantage that building backlinks is now harder because less of your competition is willing to undertake the more time-intensive process.

Quantity doesn't win here. Link quality, strength, and relevance does. If you don't embrace quality over quantity, you'll dig a deeper hole of cleaning up backlinks that you'll have to deal with later after Google penalizes you.

There is no link building checklist, since link opportunities may vary. Link building is an art as much as it is a science that requires constant tweaking. You will be required to be hyper-aware about what is happening within your industry so you can produce content and engage online. That may sound intense, but link building can be deeply gratifying when you start to see results. Be excited and get ready.

Chapter Five

Be Human

A powerful and fun way to build links is through networking. Yes, human connections. This may not initially sound like SEO, but networking is a powerful channel for growing your links if you do it with clear intentions. By building relationships and providing value, you gain trust. And with trust comes opportunities – to connect, not to sell.

But isn't the whole point to pitch people for links? No. Links are certainly the long-term benefit, but not the short-term goal. For example, I regularly network on LinkedIn. I am constantly complimented on my approach of giving without trying to sell my connections. Here's an example of the unsolicited feedback I receive:

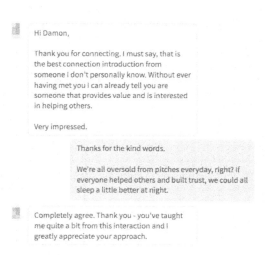

Hi Damon,

Thank you for connecting. I must say, that is the best connection introduction from someone I don't personally know. Without ever having met you I can already tell you are someone that provides value and is interested in helping others.

Very impressed.

Thanks for the kind words.

We're all oversold from pitches everyday, right? If everyone helped others and built trust, we could all sleep a little better at night.

Completely agree. Thank you - you've taught me quite a bit from this interaction and I greatly appreciate your approach.

Feedback? Great. But how's that equate to money?

Look at it this way. You can be a "hunter," always "moving" and *feel* busy, *thinking* you're making progress, constantly grinding for the kill (backlink). Or, you can be a patient "fisherman," letting *bigger and better backlinks do all the work and come to you.* All you had to do was set the bait in the form of giving away free value.

Here is an example of my giving approach on social media translating into real dollars. An unsolicited message that converted into a one-time $4,000 deal, and a few additional projects since then.

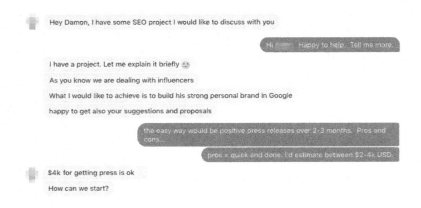

This value-added, non-salesy post lead to a *recurring* $4,000/month client.

Damon Burton

🌏 ▾

💣 VALUE BOMBS 💣

I have a free Facebook group where I drop SEO advice regularly. I've started recapping the posts throughout each month at the end.

#1 ✅ Proof that whomever says "SEO is dead" is out of touch or tunnel-visioned. Brightedge release a study showing that organic traffic makes up the MAJORITY of most websites' traffic.

https://www.facebook.com/groups/outrank/permalink
/2558438824215039/

#2 😊 Why building a process is ABSOLUTELY crucial to your success:

https://www.facebook.com/groups/outrank/permalink
/2549014831824105/

#3 ✅ Screenshots from an SEO client that that has increased their online revenue by $165,219.97, and there is still the three busiest months of the year left in 2019.

https://www.facebook.com/groups/outrank/permalink
/2571630352895886/

#4 The perfect list of plugins to optimize a Wordpress website:

https://www.facebook.com/groups/outrank/permalink
/2535087736550148/

Using this method, I've done SEO audits for billion-dollar companies, like Dollar Shave Club.

Here is another that translated into a $5,900 website and a $2,000/month recurring retainer.

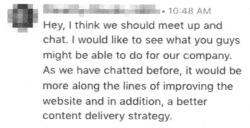

I've found that *not* selling is the best way to sell. Kindness is. I've even written about that, too.

Damon Burton
SEO National :: Published Search Engine Optimization Consultant
3d

Want to see a magic trick?

I turn kindness into money.

Recently, two businesses came to me out of desperation.

Their "web guy" burned them.

Their websites stopped taking orders, and they needed it fixed ASAP.

They asked a friend for help and were referred to me.

It was the furthest thing from convenient to take on someone else's fire. But I usually do if I can tell it's genuinely a bad situation.

I helped them out and invoiced them only $100'ish. I had to get back to my pre-interruption tasks, so I didn't even charge them extra for the urgency.

I had to get back to making sure my existing clients were taken care of.

Next day, both people called back and said something like, "I appreciate your willingness to help. Can I talk to you about this other thing..."

Both are now full-project clients, one even paying a monthly recurring retainer.

I can't tell you how many of my clients evolve from a willingness to help, but it's a lot.

Even running a marketing company, word of mouth is by far my biggest source of leads.

And half of those referrals are people that I've never charged $0.01 because I couldn't help them.

But I did point them in the right direction.

Kindness is the best form of marketing.

People remember others that treat them as a fellow human.

71 Likes · 34 Comments

👍 Like   💬 Comment   ↪ Share

📈 2,726 views of your post in the feed

In addition to kindness, people want to interact with... people. They want to do business with real humans more than faceless companies. To be human, you need to be authentic, and part of being authentic is being vulnerable.

Don't be shy. Being vulnerable is what makes people relate to you. Here is one example of a personal post that racked up 11,000+ views in less than a week.

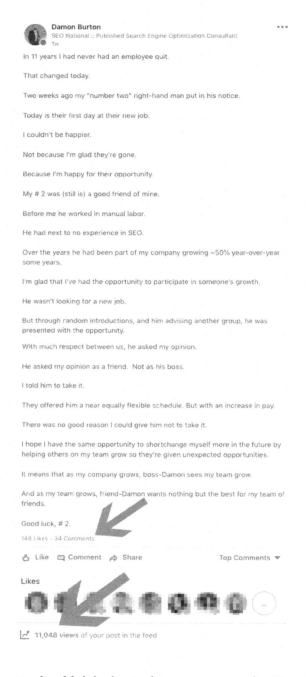

Being authentic shouldn't be limited to posts you make. You should also be authentic in the messages that you send as you make new connections.

Here is an example of the relationships that you build and the positivity that you get in return.

━━━━━━ ━━━━ • 10:41 PM

Hey, Damon, this may be the slowest ever response...I'll admit when i first got your emails i felt maybe they were sales pitches, notwithstanding your comments to the contrary...but i've read your posts and found you to be a great contributor to the community and i always look forward to reading your posts...sorry that i've not ever responded before....i hope things are going well for you, and based on your posts i think they are and that you have found a way to balance life, work and all the other things...

And another example:

━━━━ Thanks very much for meeting with me by phone today. I really appreciate that you took the time to explain so many aspects of SEO and how to select the right organization to do work for my company. I also appreciate the additional information you offered. I love learning new things and you helped me a lot today. You certainly are a generous person. I look forward to the proposal you send me. Enjoy the rest of your day. ━━━━ ☺

Another:

━━━━━━ ━━━━ 1st

Founder & Chief Executive Officer (CEO) at ━━━━ LLC.

TODAY

━━━━━━━━ • 10:07 AM

Damon I have a sporting goods company I'd like to have you do some SEO stuff on, when can we talk briefly?

More:

 3:42 PM

from my dad: "Whatever Damon did, the website is working like crazy. We keep getting emails one after the other." Yay!!!!

And more:

 • 5:20 PM

You may hear this a lot, but that was by far the most fun of an introduction I have EVER received on Linkedin. Thank you for not being so dry on social media...

I'm actually looking for SEO info. I know I need it, but it's last on my list, but I know its need to be first. If you wish to perform an SEO search I can entertain the feedback.

Blessings and thank you in advance,

More again:

 • 7:24 AM

Thanks Sir,
Your posts are always inspire me for professional growth.

 Damon Burton • 5:40 PM

Hi there. Thanks for the kind words. I appreciate it, and wish you continued success.

 • 6:46 PM

It's my pleasure

Looking forward for your guidance always.

And again:

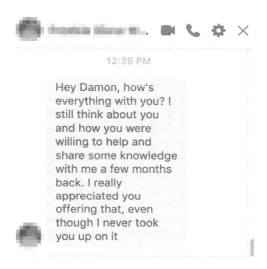

One more:

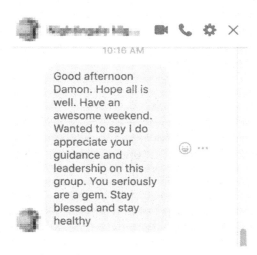

And the post that reached the largest audience hit over 200,000 views when I stopped checking after a few weeks.

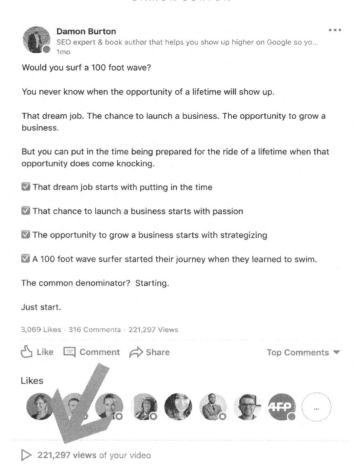

Damon Burton
SEO expert & book author that helps you show up higher on Google so yo...
1mo

Would you surf a 100 foot wave?

You never know when the opportunity of a lifetime will show up.

That dream job. The chance to launch a business. The opportunity to grow a business.

But you can put in the time being prepared for the ride of a lifetime when that opportunity does come knocking.

☑ That dream job starts with putting in the time

☑ That chance to launch a business starts with passion

☑ The opportunity to grow a business starts with strategizing

☑ A 100 foot wave surfer started their journey when they learned to swim.

The common denominator? Starting.

Just start.

3,069 Likes · 316 Comments · 221,297 Views

👍 Like   💬 Comment   ↪ Share   Top Comments ▼

Likes

▷ **221,297 views** of your video

I don't sell anything in posts like these. I give value or talk about things that I appreciate, like my wife and kids, and that keeps me top-of-mind to my audience. This strategy has lead to approximately $150,000 in new business in the first year alone in implementing it.

Some of my biggest accounts have been the result of giving away value, expecting nothing in return, only to have it come back full circle. When you offer value and are authentic to people, they trust you. And when they need a service that you provide or someone they know does, you are top-of-mind, and they'll be coming straight to you or recommending you to their friends.

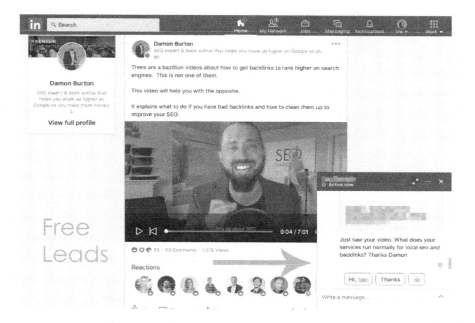

For this process to work, you must ignore previous ideas that you need to beat everyone else down to get what you want. The opposite is true. Google, social media, and other online platforms are expediting this collaborative approach like never before, and this "social currency" should be the backbone of everything you do.

SEO should be about answering questions, solving problems, and providing real value to others so that they want to share it with their friends, family, business partners, and network. You cannot do that if you skip the part about providing value.

Don't get me wrong. I understand that most of us usually start, grow, or manage a business because of financial interests. But let's look past that for a moment. Being kind can bring you rewards well beyond a financial return. For example, taking care of my team has led me to immeasurable non-financial blessings. The most recent of which was being asked to be a godfather.

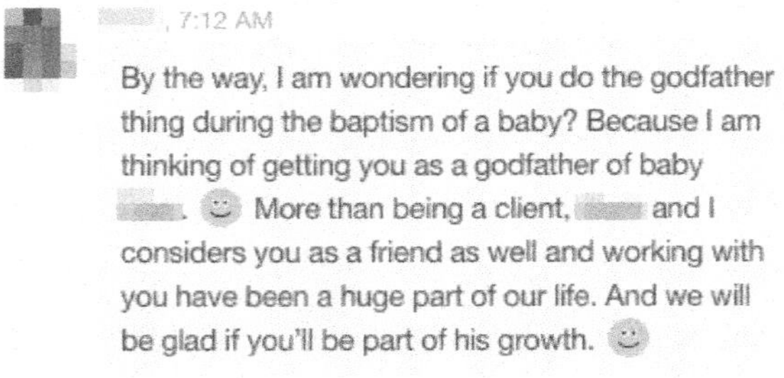
, 7:12 AM
By the way, I am wondering if you do the godfather thing during the baptism of a baby? Because I am thinking of getting you as a godfather of baby . More than being a client, and I considers you as a friend as well and working with you have been a huge part of our life. And we will be glad if you'll be part of his growth.

I've even been invited to be the guest of honor at a wedding of two of my international team members. When I couldn't make it in person due to my wife being due with our third child, they went out of their way to have me be present in the form of a life-size cardboard cutout of me that they ordered.

There are no words to quantify my appreciation for these gestures.

Chapter Six

Content? How Much and How Often?

B y now it is clear that outranking your competition takes time. Anyone promising instant success does not have your best interest at heart. Just like other things that we aspire to be, such as a Fortune 500 CEO, a doctor, a lawyer, an Olympic athlete, or raising kids (and I know a lot about the latter), SEO takes time to practice and cultivate. We learn as we go, and get better and more competent through our efforts. What we must do is begin where we are.

The more you focus your attention, build a strategy, are consistent, and practice the actions that move you towards your goal, the closer and clearer the objective becomes. SEO is a process with a powerful science behind it. You can't put a hot mess out on the internet and expect traffic and sales to just come to you. That's not how the laws of SEO work. They demand you build credibility and authority, one blog, one article, one interview, one link, and one connection at a time. But as you put these things in place, they begin to add up, and the more you do, the greater your momentum.

Often, however, after you have tackled some of the technical aspects of optimization, the task of creating original, authority-building content can feel daunting. Coming up with fresh, on-point ideas week after week soon becomes too much for the majority of us: Not just content, but unique content. Whatever you do, don't cut corners on content. Your content needs to be solid in every way. It must be useful, original, well researched, well written, insightful, properly formatted, error-free, relevant, and engaging.

Effective content is not something you can improvise very effectively. There are too many moving parts. A working plan is the glue that holds everything together. Stick with me, and I'll tell you how to research, schedule, and write effective content.

Content is not a one-and-done activity. Content must be generated continuously to ensure SEO. Why? Well, you might have heard that search engines don't rank stale websites as well when compared to sites with fresh, consistent content, and that is true. The reality is that if you aren't actively generating content, you aren't demonstrating any expertise, and thus consistently attracting new and relevant links and authority. The content on each of your pages should be full, complete, informative, and free from error. If you can't illustrate to search engines why you are different or better than your competition, why would they rank you differently or better?

As you create quality content, you will build your online credibility. You will establish a reputation as a known authority. Bloggers, podcasters, and online media outlets will begin asking you to supply your wisdom instead of you asking them to allow you to do so. When you provide value on or for their sites, lots of juicy links will begin pointing back to you. As you build that reputation, you will become a go-to source, and people will share and link to your content over time.

That sounds wonderful, doesn't it? But how do you get from relative obscurity to sought-after expert status? It is part business strategy, part public relations, part marketing, and all SEO. Links or no links, you need to put in the time to promote your business. Good links are just the icing on the cake.

To build solid content that acquires links, you must have clarity about what you can share with the world that is original (enough) and compelling (enough) to capture people's attention and make them want to know more. When you know your core topic, that will support the keywords that you want to rank for. Then you need a set of more granular topics to support your core topic, and you explore those granular topics from every angle imaginable, week after week, after week.

Don't be surprised if your audience is a little quiet or entirely non-existent at first. Just stay with it every week, creating content, solidifying your message, tying into current events, and popular searches whenever and wherever possible to piggyback on the tide of public interest. Content is a process, but if you are focused, diligent, and consistent, it is a process that will pay you back in spades.

I am going to share my "secret sauce" for building an effective 52-week content calendar to streamline your content creation. You can steal it from me if you like – step-by-step. Or you can cherry-pick ideas and adapt as you need for your industry and website.

What I know is that the clearest path to building content that works starts with a framework of ideas. That's the hardest part for most of us. Once you have that, the rest of what you must do falls neatly into place.

On the next page, you can see what a sample 52-week content calendar looks like. The topics in this example calendar are not necessarily industry-specific but are probably better suited for a corporate-style business. Regardless of the actual topics, you will see the simplicity of this calendar and realize that the ability to streamline content creation is not as hard as you once thought.

January			
Week 1	topic	New Year's Resolution for Business	
	notes	Talk about how we're all excited to do great things this year, hence, we make New Year's Resolutions. Help business owners commit to accomplishing their goals this year.	
Week 2	topic	National Thank You Month	
	notes	If you're an entrepreneur wanting to express gratitude to your loyal customers or clients and employees, here are some creative ways to do it.	
Week 3	topic	Hire Contractors Before Going Full-time: A Good Idea?	
	notes	Talk about the benefits of hiring contractors instead of full-timers. This is mostly applicable for businesses with a tight budget.	
Week 4	topic	Get the Right Consultant for your Business Growth	
	notes	Expert opinions and guidance can help your business soar. How to find the right contractor for your business?	

Backup Alternate	topic	Pros and Cons of Flexible Work Schedules
	notes	There are advantages and disadvantages when allowing employees to work flexible schedules. Calculate if the advantages outweigh the disadvantages.
February		
Week 1	topic	Better Presentation Skills for Business Owners
	notes	For entrepreneurs and small business owners who rely on presentations to land big client accounts, a bad presentation can be the difference between success and failure. Here are some tips.
Week 2	topic	How Businesses Can Take Advantage of Valentine's Day
	notes	Valentine's Day isn't just about "stuff." Some consumers tend to treat their loved ones to experiences such as dinner at a romantic restaurant or a movie night. How can business owners take advantage of this?
Week 3	topic	Why Encourage your Employees to have a Side Project
	notes	Explain the pros and cons of encouraging employees to have side projects.
Week 4	topic	Productivity Tools for Entrepreneurs
	notes	Feature some cool tools/equipment that help entrepreneurs boost productivity.
Backup Alternate	topic	Business Plan Mistakes You Should Avoid
	notes	Every business should have a plan. Some entrepreneurs, however, make business plans that only lead them to failures, or worse, bankruptcy. Here are some common business plan mistakes and how to avoid them.
March		
Week 1	topic	Read Across America Day
	notes	In light of Read Across America Day, highlight the benefits of reading daily. Feature some good business books.
Week 2	topic	How to Make Your Customers Choose Your Business
	notes	Every business owner thinks their business is unique. Be realistic, what is so unique about your empire? It's not about your product, it's about you, your culture, and your relationships. Here are tips to attract customer to your business.

Week 3	topic	The Importance of Goal Setting
	notes	There's some impressive science to back up goal setting. And yet it's something we're rarely taught or encouraged to do. Talk about how goal setting can be beneficial to any endeavor, especially business.
Week 4	topic	Tips to Generate Sales Leads
	notes	Highlight proven methods to generate sales leads.
Backup Alternate	topic	Can SEO Help Your Struggling Business?
	notes	Businesses small and large alike—especially struggling ones—can benefit from an SEO marketing campaign. Explain what SEO can do to a struggling business.
April		
Week 1	topic	Jargons to "avoid" and "to use" in the Workplace
	notes	List some of the worst words to use in a workplace and other buzzwords that are acceptable.
Week 2	topic	Myths about Startup Businesses
	notes	Highlight the myths about startup businesses. What are some people used to believe is true, but not even close in reality.
Week 3	topic	Earth Day
	notes	Talk about the essence of Earth Day. Then encourage readers to raise awareness. Here are effective ways.
Week 4	topic	Reasons Your Online Business is not Getting Traction
	notes	Discuss why some online businesses never gain traction. What are the reasons? How can they get traction?
Backup Alternate	topic	How Technology is Changing Small Businesses
	notes	Technology impacts the way small businesses raise capital. It has opened doors for talented entrepreneurs who otherwise wouldn't have had access to funding. Write about the role of technology in progressing small businesses.
May		
Week 1	topic	Types of Business Strategies
	notes	Any company can use a number of business strategies, depending on its situation. Highlight these strategies and explain when to apply them.
Week 2	topic	How To Give Effective Feedback
	notes	Not giving feedback, especially when it's necessary to address unacceptable behavior, has consequences. Create an action plan to provide critical, beneficial feedback. Here are some tips.

Week 3	topic	An Effective Way to Connect With Customers
	notes	Suggest effective ways to connect with customers and build lasting relationships that will keep them loyal.
Week 4	topic	Signs Your Client is Happy No More
	notes	Highlight the warning signs that entrepreneurs should recognize that a client might be planning to go in a different direction. How to win them back and make them clients for life?
Backup Alternate	topic	When to Quit Your Business According to Seth Godin
	notes	Quitting is ok. Here are reasons to start fresh.
June		
Week 1	topic	How to Know if Your Business Idea Will Work
	notes	You might have the most amazing business idea ever, but how do you know if it will actually work? Here's how to tell.
Week 2	topic	What Benefits to Gift Your Employees?
	notes	Suggest some enticing perks entrepreneurs should consider giving their employees.
Week 3	topic	How to Make Meetings More Effective
	notes	Although most meetings are unproductive, there are ways to make them effective. Here's what you need to do.
Week 4	topic	Time Management That Works For You
	notes	The problem is we tend to use time management methods from other people, which may not be the right methods for us. Educate readers about the importance of using a time management system that works for them.
Backup Alternate	topic	The Importance of Knowing Your Personality Type in Business
	notes	Highlight the reasons why it can be beneficial to determine our personality type before we start a business. What are the pros and cons? What are some personality traits that can help business owners?
July		
Week 1	topic	Fourth of July
	notes	Talk about the activities associated with Independence Day. Then transition into providing marketing ideas for the Fourth of July. How businesses can take advantage of the holiday?

Week 2	topic	Online vs. Offline Business: Which is Good For You?
	notes	What are the factors to consider when choosing between online or offline business? Each has pros and cons that should be considered.
Week 3	topic	Social Media Mistakes That Can Hurt Your Company
	notes	Social media is also a great way to build up a business, but it can tear it down again just as quickly. Here are some mistakes to avoid.
Week 4	topic	Staying Focused is Crucial for Business, Here's Why
	notes	Emphasize the importance of focus when running a business. Suggest tips on how to stay focused during hard times.
Backup Alternate	topic	The Importance of a Mentor
	notes	A mentor can be a difference maker in your career, business, and life. Explain the benefits of having a mentor and suggest ways on how to choose the right one.
August		
Week 1	topic	Maintain a Healthy Business Relationship
	notes	Maintaining healthy business relationships is critical for success, and that includes knowing when to leave them. Here's what entrepreneurs should keep in mind.
Week 2	topic	Changes in the Workplace: What to Expect
	notes	Managing change means managing people's fear. Change is natural and good, but people's reaction to change is unpredictable and irrational. It can be managed if done right. Here's what you need to do.
Week 3	topic	Lazy Employee? Here's how to deal with it
	notes	If an employee is not motivated to perform at the expected level, it must be addressed. Depending on the answer, the employer can then take appropriate action. Share ways to deal with unmotivated employees.
Week 4	topic	Bad SEO Tactics That Can Hurt Entrepreneurs
	notes	Highlight some BAD SEO tactics that can hurt entrepreneurs. What are the signs that your SEO tactics are causing your business harm?
Backup Alternate	topic	How to Become a Better Decision-Maker According to Warren Buffet and Jeff Bezos
	notes	Entrepreneurs must be good at decision making. Otherwise, they put their businesses in danger. Discuss various decision-making models.

September			
Week 1	topic	Expanding Business to Another State	
	notes	Talk about the importance of understanding the ins and outs of expanding a business into a new state. What are the pros and cons?	
Week 2	topic	Reasons Your Employees Hate You	
	notes	The one factor that signifies an ineffective management is that employees hate their boss. Highlight the reasons why.	
Week 3	topic	The Importance of Engaging Workplace	
	notes	Developing an engaged workplace requires a combination of people, programs and policies. Here's how to do it.	
Week 4	topic	Different Ways to Grow an Online Business	
	notes	For those who are just getting started, make sure all the elements for your online success are in place. Talk about some proven (or counterintuitive) ways to grow an online brand.	
Backup Alternate	topic	How Entrepreneurs Stay Organized	
	notes	Provide proven ways to help busy entrepreneurs stay organized. Is it possible? How to deal with chaos in business and life?	
October			
Week 1	topic	Seasonal Hiring Things to Consider	
	notes	Hiring extra help for the holiday season? Consider these crucial things when looking for temp workers.	
Week 2	topic	Reasons Some Businesses Fail While Others Succeed	
	notes	Some people start one successful business after another while others fail to succeed. What happened? Here are some known reasons.	
Week 3	topic	Signs You're Not Fit For Entrepreneurship	
	notes	Many people want to start a business. But not everyone has what it takes. What are the signs you're not cut out for entrepreneurship?	
Week 4	topic	Leadership vs. Management	
	notes	Compare and contrast leadership and management. What is the difference? Which one is better when building a long-term business?	
Backup Alternate	topic	How to Build Credibility	
	notes	Establishing credibility doesn't happen over night, but here are some ways to expedite the process	

November		
Week 1	topic	Traits of Effective Leadership
	notes	What are the traits of an effective leader? Discuss how good leadership can be a determining factor for business success.
Week 2	topic	Veterans Day: Business Ideas for Veterans
	notes	Provide ideas for veterans who are planning to start a business. What type of businesses that fit their skill-set? How can they penetrate the market?
Week 3	topic	Cyber Monday
	notes	Take advantage of Cyber Monday. Suggest online shopping or online selling tips.
Week 4	topic	Business Ideas for Winter
	notes	Suggest business ideas that are practical for winter.
Backup Alternate	topic	How Small Businesses Can Take Advantage of Mobile Apps
	notes	Being mobile is not just about having a mobile-friendly website. It means connecting with on-the-go customers and employees. Here's how small businesses can take advantage of mobile apps.
December		
Week 1	topic	Tips to Prepare Your Business for Christmas Season
	notes	Christmas is about connecting with the people around us, giving thanks and celebrating. Expect sales surge. Suggest tips on how entrepreneurs can prepare for Christmas season.
Week 2	topic	How to avoid having "Drainers" in your Business
	notes	Does your business have "drainers" – people whose negativity drains everyone else's energy and drags the business down? Suggest tips on how to fix business energy drains.
Week 3	topic	Managing Remote Employees
	notes	How to manage, motivate, and retain remote employees? What can you do to maintain productivity?
Week 4	topic	The Importance of Choosing the Right Business Partner
	notes	Before looking for a business partner, contemplate whether you even need one at all. Discuss the advantages of choosing the right business partner and the consequences of picking the wrong one.
Backup Alternate	topic	Business Trends on the Rise
	notes	Looking at the new year ahead, discuss rising trends in your industry.

Pretty straightforward, right? Once you have your 52-week content calendar in place, you can pre-produce content well in advance to outpace your competition. To make it even easier, download your free copy of this 52-week content calendar outline at:

www.seonational.com/free-seo-templates/

We agree now about the importance of content. But what do you do if you're not the writing type, despite knowing its importance? Here are some options to help you source freelance writers.

1. Fiverr - seonational.com/fiverr

   You may already be familiar with Fiverr. Just be sure to quality control Fiverr produced content. Otherwise, you could unknowingly be placing content that was just copied from another website onto yours, which Google penalizes. And we'll talk more about that later.

2. Iwriter - seonational.com/writers

   Iwriter lets you set your price and pay for higher-rated, more effective writers. This can help minimize the issue of low-quality content that may come from Fiverr.

It's also worth noting that if you've had SEO done in the past, then it's a good idea to audit that content before you start building up new content. The benefits of reviewing old content are to confirm that any previous SEO company didn't source (or flat out steal) content from another website and post it on yours, which may now be doing more SEO harm than good. Here are two useful resources to audit your internal content.

1. Copyscape.com - Copyscape can help you identify content that may have originally been sourced from other websites. Maybe you hired a copywriter and now realize that they may not have provided original content.

2. SiteLiner.com - Maybe you excessively duplicated your content or used keyword stuffing tactics from SEO's wild-wild-west days. Site Liner will help you compare pages on your website against other pages on your website to identify excessively repeated content.

Now that your content is cleaned up and you've started writing new, unique, optimized pieces of content, repurpose it. Since you already put in the time to research the topic and create compelling content, don't reinvent the wheel. Repurpose blog text into an infographic. Then, further repurpose the content into a video for YouTube, which is one of the most visible platforms on the internet.

Whether Google admits favoritism or not for owning YouTube, their videos rank coincidentally well on Google.

If you're camera-shy, don't let that stop you from creating videos. You can use visuals instead of yourself on-screen. Or, use a software that will create a video for you without you having to be on-screen. The software that I recommend for this, and use myself, is called Vidnami:

www.seonational.com/videos

In the content section of your video, you can include your blog text as the transcript of your video, which offers even more layers of search engine friendly content. To come full circle, after your video is loaded to YouTube, embed that same video back on your blog post that you sourced the video text from.

Combine your video, infographic, or other repurposed content and stack it within your blog post to create a content-rich page that is more diversified than your competitor's text-only blog post.

You can even consider repurposing your blog for Quora, Medium, or LinkedIn to leverage those audiences. Each of these platforms helps raise awareness of your SEO-influenced content and attracts a loyal following.

I am well aware that the idea of producing content may not resonate with a lot of people. Especially those that feel blogs are irrelevant to their business model. I hear them dismiss the entire process before they even try it with statements like, "Oh, blogs don't apply to me – I'm a dry cleaner (or feng shui consultant, or graphic designer, or any other business you can imagine)." If that sounds like what you are thinking, then I encourage you to expand your understanding of a blog. There is, hands down, no single better platform for you to showcase your expertise than a blog. No one can censor your content to minimize the value that you can present to your potential customers.

If you are a dry cleaner, talk about how to care for and protect clothing – or branch out into wardrobe success tips, and environmental issues. If you are a graphic designer, discuss design trends, critique websites and logos, and provide tips and how-tos. In other words, regardless of the business model, there is powerful, useful, authority-building content you can (and should) be putting out regularly to be seen and recognized as a thought leader.

The other obstacle that mystifies me is the overly-modest business owner. This individual says, "I don't have anything new to say." Sometimes it makes you question why they became business owners in the first place if they hold their own offerings in such low regard. And if they feel that way, imagine what their customers think. No wonder these individuals' websites are invisible on search engines. If you want to rank uniquely, you have to be unique.

You don't have to create or repurpose your content using all of these options, but doing so allows you to have a greater potential footprint in search results. In addition to having your website show up, you may also have an image and video show up. How much more credible would you look with three top-ranking results versus just one?

If you have any desire to outrank your competitors, be of service to your ideal audience, and don't withhold what makes you unique. SEO is no place for low self-esteem or false modesty. Likewise, you don't have to be arrogant. Just be willing to share content that your audience will find useful in some way.

If you always keep your customers' needs at the forefront of your awareness, you cannot help but grow your authority as a result. You are the expert. Your audience needs you.

Chapter Seven

Time is Money

According to Search Engine Land and data from a Forrester study, "71% of consumers begin their journeys by using a search engine to discover new products and services, and 74% reported using a search engine for consideration and purchasing."

https://searchengineland.com/
value-search-across-modern-consumer-decision-journey-270021

If you're not showing up in those results, you are not only not in the race; you are not even on the field. It doesn't matter what industry you are in. Once you begin to recognize the priceless nature of your online reputation, the next natural question is: *How do I get to the top of Google?*

The answer is: a lot of work, and done continuously.

As with most business activities, if you want to make money, you have to invest money (or time). Many boot-strapped startups don't want to hear this and are continually searching for a cheap or free quick-fix to their cash-poor situation. There is no such thing as free marketing, and SEO is no exception to this rule.

That being said, as you read this book, you are beginning to understand very clearly why good SEO costs what it does. Boot-strapped startups have their place, and many of us, including myself, have gotten our start as one. But to have access to SEO that genuinely helps businesses grow, there are no cheap or free routes.

It all boils down to one thing: solid SEO takes time – and a lot of it. Whether it is your time, my time, or some other SEO company's time, that time has a dollar value attached to it. You need to decide whether you are willing to spend your time on SEO or pay someone else to spend their time on your behalf. If the answer is neither, then, my friend, you are not yet ready for SEO.

To decide if you are ready to take the SEO leap, ask yourself these questions:

1. Can I generate enough business based on word of mouth and referrals to grow at the rate I want to?
2. If your answer to #1 was "no," are you going to invest in a sales team and a live presence, focus on online visibility, or all of the above?
3. If online visibility is a priority, how many customers do I want to reach, and how much is each one worth to me?
4. How much capital *am I able* to invest to reach more customers?
5. How much capital *do I need* to invest to reach more customers?

It is important to note that questions 4 and 5 are not the same question. If your answer to #4 is a lesser value than #5, you have a cash flow problem, and that must be dealt with before anything else. Even more importantly, there are no right or wrong answers to any of these questions. The only mistake you can make here is to not ask them of yourself and your business, which some companies never do.

Okay. So what does SEO cost? Before we dive into how to quantify the cost of good SEO, let's check one more time if you really need it.

Many SEO experts will tell you that to compete online that you must have SEO. That is not true.

What? An SEO myself saying that SEO is not always necessary? Exactly. While I love taking on new clients, I also have a conscience and like sleeping at night. My company's success has primarily been built on the backs of honesty and transparency. If SEO isn't right for someone, or at least not at the moment, then they deserve an honest answer.

Millions of small businesses have little or no SEO – like a family-owned business down the street, a consultant who works from home and has built enough business to stay busy, but has no intentions of growing any larger until the kids are out of school - maybe. They are perfectly happy where they are. And that's a beautiful thing to find that happiness.

But if you want to spread your message further or grow your revenue more, then SEO may be exactly what you need. So, how much is it going to cost? The answer will depend on several factors:

- **Size and Scope of Work:** The larger the business, competitive the industry, more comprehensive the offerings, or broader the reach desired, the more time and effort (and, therefore, more cost) will need to be invested towards driving positive SEO results.

- **CMS (Content Management System):** Some CMS are more SEO-friendly than others, allowing you to optimize more efficiently, faster. Likewise, some CMS can be more painstaking and slow to work with, costing more time, which requires more money.

- **Type of SEO Provider:** Besides full-service SEO firms like SEO National, who work on a retainer basis, others offer hourly consulting or even fixed pricing. We will look at examples of typical pricing structures from each of these types of providers, but as with everything, there is a direct correlation between price and progress.

- **Previous SEO Efforts:** If a business had SEO done in the past, this could affect the cost of future SEO significantly, and unfavorably. The reason for this is that if a business is seeking another SEO provider, it is rarely because the previous provider gave them great results. Poor results are almost always because outdated or bad SEO strategies were used. This means that the new SEO company has to spend time cleaning up the mess. Due to this cleanup, potential Google penalties, and lost revenue, cheap SEO often ends up costing more than had you just done good, "more expensive" SEO in the first place.

It's fair to say that if a business wants effective SEO, it either pays now or pay *more* later. So if it is tempting to cut corners until the funds are available for real SEO, then it is better to wait until full cash flow is on hand.

This leads us to the elephant in the room – what sort of investment are we talking about here?

At the writing of this book, there are several pricing models, with a wide range of investments.

Basic SEO: Typical SEO costs start at $750 per month, or less, as a retainer for smaller businesses working with an equally small SEO agency offering a limited range of services. While this may sound like a great deal, the most important word here is "limited." Limited services yield limited results. While the strategy may be reliable, the efforts within that strategy are not executed frequently enough to elevate your website's ranking very much, if at all.

Full-service SEO: On the higher end of the retainer pricing model, full-service SEO firms typically charge between $2500 and $10,000 per month. These full-service agencies offer not only site structure improvements, competitive analysis, and link building services, but also time-intensive content creation and distribution. Clients pay a recurring monthly retainer in exchange for an agreed-upon list of services, including competitive analysis, keyword research, page structure improvements, content creation and distribution, regular analytics reports, and overall optimization. These firms operate much like a PR agency, helping create a constant stream of positive brand awareness signals for search engines to pick up on, which are crucial to SEO success. This is why this model is the most popular and provides the highest SEO ROI, because it is structured specifically around the uniqueness of the individual website, its goals, and precisely what content/assets are needed to achieve those goals.

Obviously, not every business is ready to invest $30,000-$120,000+ annually to establish reliable SEO results. For this reason, other options carry tremendous appeal and can be a reasonable bridge to the standard retainer model. These bridge options can be useful to a degree, so long as the business understands what they will ultimately be paying for, and what to look for in a short-term solution so they don't harm their long-term potential.

Contract search engine optimization: Contract SEO services are a common SEO starting point when smaller budgets are a factor. They help with fundamental SEO components such as site structure audits, cost-per-word copywriting, and backlink portfolio audits. As a result, contract services by reputable providers get a site set up for success at a one-time price between $2,500-$18,000. Because of this wide price range, it is vital that the SEO company provides a clear outline and specific costs to their client, and that the customer fully understands the scope and limits of what they are purchasing. Otherwise, these efforts can add up quickly and include no long-term strategy, which is a crucial piece of maintaining SEO rankings.

Project-based pricing: Buying SEO à la carte is a common practice. Much like the Contract SEO option, this limited approach has equally limited results. If a business uses this model to execute the full range of SEO services, they are likely to spend just as much, or more, than a retainer would cost them for the same work. As an example, a single SEO project handled in this manner can range between $1,000 to $30,000 but provides no on-going services to scale your SEO visibility as search engine algorithms evolve.

Hourly SEO consulting: $100-300/hr. For businesses intending to perform their SEO internally, it can be helpful to bring in an SEO consultant, as needed. While this arrangement does not eliminate the burden of time-consuming effort required, this is at least an option to guide a business down the right SEO path towards success.

Different SEO pricing options are not necessarily mutually exclusive, and most SEO firms offer several or all of them. For example, a business might enter into a monthly retainer, purchase a contract service, and engage in a special project with the agency, thus entering three of the payment models simultaneously. It all depends on the potential profits to be gained by the customer to narrow down which option makes sense.

Buyer Beware

Because of the general lack of understanding about the science of SEO, and the rampant cultural appetite for instant gratification, an entire industry of SEO scam artists has sprung up.

Unfortunately, as in any industry, some people in SEO are not the most honest, and they promise to get you on page one of Google overnight. This is a tempting sales pitch but not a feasible one. There is no such thing as instant gratification in SEO. And for added emphasis, if someone calls you and says they are from Google, hang up. Google doesn't call anyone to solicit services. Especially not SEO.

These scammers are preying on the under-informed, who are looking for a cheaper, easier way. The results are mediocre at best, and devastating at worst. It can waste precious financial resources of a business, and, by association, it undercuts the reputation of an otherwise reputable industry.

For real success, you should be asking your potential SEO company questions. If and when you see sales pitches that include the red flags that I list below, run as far and fast as you can.

- **Guarantees.** The SEO industry is continually changing and evolving. Due to a large number of variables involved, specific guarantees are dicey at best. Any reputable SEO knows this and will be transparent with you about why guaranteeing specifics is merely an educated guess. Instead, a good SEO will speak in "averages" and time frames. (i.e., "Most clients rank within X time frame, but it could take as long as Y.")

- **Instant results.** As with anything promising immediate results, there is usually something else that is at risk of being seriously harmed. SEO is no different. To get seemingly instant rankings, agencies would likely have to use tactics that violate Google's policies. While these strategies might work briefly, the collateral damage when the search engines catch on (and they will, sooner or later) end with your website being banished to invisibility. Regaining rank and credibility after such "instant results" can take months, even years.

- **A monopoly on top rankings.** This is the Holy Grail of SEO. Yes, the goal is top rankings, but total domination for *every* keyword imaginable is unrealistic. Considering the number of websites fighting for top spots, even if you are doing everything right, only one will walk away with the gold. Based on logic alone, this makes no sense to promise, but it doesn't stop many from trying it anyway.

- **Backlinks galore.** We discussed the problem with bad links earlier, and yet, the temptation remains to cut corners, go for quantity over quality, and accept highly questionable link building as the road to SEO glory. I have yet to see anyone who went this route live to tell about it without some battle scars from their favorite search engine.

- **Costs lower than $500/month.** It is fascinating how willing people are to waste money for a "great deal" instead of paying a little more for quality, even when the stakes are incredibly high. Next, I will explain why SEO costs what it does. For now, know that anyone charging less than $500 per month is either an amateur or is taking your money and running and not providing enough ethical effort to generate real SEO results. And that's for a non-competitive industry. SEO costs for a more competitive industry should easily start at $1,000+. Either way, the risk is too great.

SEO is not a mindless endeavor. Effective SEO aims to structure your site so that it resonates with both search engines and users. Copywriting skills and quality website design are the prices of entry. In other words, whoever is building your SEO needs to grasp what resonates with your customers. This is no cookie-cutter activity.

Furthermore, the more websites there are in your industry, the longer that SEO is going to take. Worse, you have to compete for rankings against websites that are *not* even in your industry. For example, search Google for a word or phrase that you'd want to rank for. What results show up? Chances are that half of the results that you have to fight against include a mix of results that don't offer a product or service that directly competes with yours. But that doesn't matter because those websites are in your way.

It's not uncommon to hear that what used to take six months to rank now takes more than a year or two. For really competitive industries, it is not unrealistic to take several years to rank. Knowing that SEO is a slow play, hopefully, it becomes obvious that you must prepare well in advance – not one of corporate culture's native strong suits. If you're not mentally committed to fully completing all that I've started to outline for an effective SEO strategy, and what remains to be discussed, then you might as well save your time and money and not even begin.

This long-term planning requires plenty of research. You'll need to study your industry, size up the competition, decide on keywords, and much more.

At this point, it can be tempting to cut corners and cut budgets, but don't be fooled. That temptation can undercut everything you are trying to achieve.

SEO is not a guessing game. It is a science, which means it delivers proven results. Improving rankings and increasing conversions improves as a result of many factors. These factors build on each other and only show real progress when they have had a chance to gather sufficient momentum.

To help illustrate why patience is key with SEO, let's look at the time frames of one common SEO strategy, submitting a press release to Google News.

You've just released your newest widget, and you want to tell the world about it. The clock is now ticking, and the process looks like this:

- It takes you a day or two to draft your press release.
- You share your press release with colleagues in hopes of feedback.
- Days go by as you await feedback.
- Feedback comes in, and you spend days revising.

A week or two has now gone by.

- You finally submit your press release.
- Another day or two goes by before it gets approved and distributed.
- Another day goes by for the news to syndicate.
- Another day goes by for Google to index the news.
- A few days go by for Google to digest the news and decide if any rankings should be adjusted as a result.
- More time goes by, and, finally, Google adjusts rankings based on your announcement, if at all this round.

Those few weeks that just went by are for one single press release. Now, multiply that equation by several other types of content to be written, designed, or distributed regularly to gain SEO momentum:

- blogging daily/weekly
- creating and distributing multimedia

- videos
- infographics
- other rich media or image-based assets
- getting other websites to feature your product/service/news
  - backlinks
  - citations/mentions

And that's assuming that you know what topics you're even going to write or design assets for. Often, the time spent researching topics takes significantly longer than actually writing or designing the piece. But if you follow the content calendar outline that was provided earlier, you should have a good head start.

It's easy to see the intensive effort and skill required for SEO to be effective, and why no one should get caught up in a sales pitch that promotes expedited SEO. It doesn't exist. Someone has to do the work, and that either costs you time or you pay for someone else's.

SEO's Big Payoff

While other forms of online marketing may have a quicker return on investment, SEO tends to have the largest return, if given sufficient time. With other types of advertising, if you want to increase your leads, you have to increase your budget, and a 200% increase in ad spending may yield as little as a 1% lift in sales. That's not a very good return. What's worse, if you need to tighten up your budget, then you end up decreasing your sales even further.

The benefit of SEO is that you're building a legacy form of sales generation. Once your efforts snowball and start to bring in business, it's only going to continue to grow. Best of all, it won't fade away any time soon.

"Return on investment" is not just a fluffy term, even though "ROI" is thrown around everywhere these days. It should be a very quantifiable dollar value, and one every business should understand, not only for SEO but every other investment they make.

To measure anticipated SEO ROI, you need to know the following:

1. Your site's current monthly traffic
2. The conversion rate of the site
3. Average value of a sale/lead

An important note here is that if you don't have any data before starting SEO, you can't effectively predict the anticipated ROI. SEO can still skyrocket your business. It's just harder to forecast. And if your transactions occur offline, it can take some trial and error to quantify your sales that originated from SEO accurately, but it can eventually be measured. For the sake of simplicity, we will assume that you have historical data, and you are handling some sort of transaction/lead/conversion that can be measured online.

If your startup site currently has only five visitors a day, but SEO can increase that by an easy-to-do 1,300 monthly visits, and the conversion rate is 3% with an average sale of $247, then forecasted monthly revenue would look like this:

(1300 x 3%) = 39 sales x $247 per sale = $9,633 in revenue.

If an SEO retainer is $2,500/month, and it takes one year for SEO to gain enough momentum to provide a return, your initial investment would be $30,000. Naturally, that initial investment could be heart-stopping to look at for a small business. However, SEO would need just over three months to pay it all back. ($30,000 investment divided by $9,633 in monthly revenue driven by SEO = 3.11 months). After you recoup your initial investment, the rest is easy money.

Every case is different, but this is the temptation in SEO. It is why so many businesses praise search engine optimization, and it is also why it is not cheap. You can't buy the investment property until you have accumulated a down payment, and the same principle applies to SEO. So take your situation, plug in your numbers, and see what SEO could do for you.

Clearly, the math shows that even if your ROI falls short of any initial estimate, you are still likely to make your money back and experience exponential returns as you continue. This applies only when SEO is done correctly and consistently. It also makes it crystal clear how trying to cut costs upfront with $200 SEO isn't worth your money. Any too-good-to-be-true SEO simply cannot be providing enough value to drive you results.

This means that for some small or startup businesses affording SEO is often not an option. This then causes them to go the Do-It-Yourself route. I believe it is possible for a business, big or small, to be successful with their own in-house SEO efforts. The question is: at what cost? The time required to do the SEO work is, at the very least, a full-time employee's salary. Which is more valuable to you? Your time or your money?

It's important to remember in SEO that what works for one website may not work for others. The reason is that every business has a different competitive landscape, which is similar to how various financial investment opportunities have higher or lower risk and reward conditions.

SEO and a 401(k) plan may not seem to belong in the same category, but you might be surprised at their similarities. Educating yourself on how to take advantage of your 401(k) to the fullest will be in your best interest. The same pertains to SEO. This is why, like your retirement planning, diversification in SEO is essential.

Everyone's heard the phrase "don't put all of your eggs in one basket." With a 401(k), you should diversify where your funds go to minimize risk. Avoid focusing your investments in one industry, even if it is making a lot of money today. With a 401(k), your investment portfolio should include large-cap, small-cap, bonds, cash on hand, and index funds. The same can be said for having a well-rounded SEO strategy. Things could change quickly, and once-thriving opportunities could vanish tomorrow, causing you to lose everything you had previously gained.

Investing in the future is a no-brainer. The earlier you start, the brighter your future will look—for both SEO and your 401(k). Financial advisors continually remind people not to delay participating in their 401(k) plan, even if they feel they can't afford it. Time is the best guarantee that retirement goals will work, so the sooner you start contributing, the better off you will be down the road. Due to compounding gains, anything you can deposit is better than nothing.

The same applies to SEO, where some website owners may feel that they cannot afford the expense. However, the sooner that you embrace SEO, the earlier you can start collecting dividends.

Chapter Eight

SEO Myths

There's an old saying, "You don't know what you don't know." That has never been truer than with search engine optimization. In the mad race to hack search engines, which is just another way of saying "cheat a little to get ahead," the SEO landscape has become littered with half-truths, misrepresentations, myths, and outright lies. While I want to believe that the perpetrators of these myths mean well and don't know any better, I know many of them are taking your money and running, doing real damage to the under-informed.

It can be nearly impossible for a novice to tell what will work and what won't when it comes to SEO strategies. In an upcoming chapter titled "25 Questions," I will help you see through the smoke and mirrors of SEO to tell the difference between the good guys and the bad. Until then, a good rule of thumb is to assume that if it sounds too good to be true, then it probably is.

Below are several common and persistent SEO myths that keep surfacing, which I will take the time to debunk – hopefully once and for all.

Myth #1
You Must Submit Your Website to Google

Search engine optimization used to require webmasters to submit their website to search engines, so the engine knew it existed. Search engine bots would then crawl the site to decide if and how to rank the website. Times have changed, and search engines can find a website on their own now. Paying for search engine submissions is no different than burning your money with a lighter, especially since Google discontinued their tool to submit websites in July of 2018.

https://searchengineland.com/google-to-stop-supporting-public-url-submissions-to-its-search-index-302571

Myth #2
Meta Keywords Matter

Meta Keyword tags (not to be confused with other meta tags, like meta descriptions) used to be an important part of the SEO process. Mile-long lists of keywords were a common strategy to try and improve a website's ranking. Stuffing any and every combination of a keyword was the name of the game. It looked something like this.

> <meta name="keywords" content="keyword 1, keyword 2, keyword 3, keyword 4, keyword 5, keyword 6, keyword 7, keyword 8, keyword 9, keyword 10, keyword 11, keyword 12, keyword 13, keyword 14, keyword 15, keyword 16, keyword 17, keyword 18, keyword 19...">

Not so much, nowadays. With this meta tag being spammed and keyword-stuffed, it forced Google to drop Meta Keywords as a ranking factor as far back as 2009.

www.seonational.com/google-meta-keywords/

Myth #3
Keyword Stuffing Makes a Tasty Side Dish

Speaking of keyword stuffing, it's a common misconception that stuffing keywords over and over within your content is a relevant SEO hack. Part of that SEO myth that refuses to go away is that "keyword density" rules the day.

Keyword density is calculated by comparing the number of SEO targeted keywords mentioned within a page to the overall total of words on that page.

This misunderstanding leads people to stuff keywords over and over into a page to convince search engines of the site's relevance. However, keyword stuffing is now proven to be ineffective as search engine algorithms can quickly see through this technique. Google has even gone on the record to give examples of keyword stuffing.

https://support.google.com/webmasters/answer/66358

- Repeating the same words or phrases so often that it sounds unnatural.
- Blocks of text listing cities and states a webpage is trying to rank for.
- Attempting to hide mass-produced text by using a white letter color over a white page background.

Myth #4
Recycled Content is Better for the World

Quantity isn't all that matters for links, and the same applies to content. Back in the early 2000's, copying content was a common SEO strategy for some people. The idea helped the lazy or uncreative increase the number of times keywords showed up on their websites, which contributed to the previously discussed keyword density. It is also a modern-day version of plagiarism, and, as of February 2011, Google's Panda algorithm aims to weed out sites that copy or primarily recycle content from other websites.

Google Panda

From Wikipedia, the free encyclopedia

Google Panda is a major change to Google's search results ranking algorithm that was first released in February 2011. The change aimed to lower the rank of "low-quality sites" or "thin sites",[1] in particular "content farms",[2] and return higher-quality sites near the top of the search results.

If Google's algorithms detect an excessive amount of duplicate content, the search engine will decide on its own which site deserves credit, and will penalize the other website(s).

Myth #5
Longer Titles Are Better

Writing lengthy, overly-optimized page titles is a common mistake of SEO beginners. Why is stuffing titles an amateur move, other than the obvious? Because Google tends to hide letters and characters in titles that run longer than 55 to 70'ish characters, cutting off the message that you're trying to communicate while stuffing. I say "70'ish" because Google no longer displays words in a search result based on a max number of letters. Instead, words in a search result are cut off based on how many pixels wide they are. What does that mean? The letter "W" is a lot wider than the letter "I," so the *letters* within your words will impact how many actual words you can display.

Part of the debate about title length has been the confusion between optimizing page titles for search engines versus for social media shareability. They are not the same thing. For SEO, title tags should generally follow these guidelines:

- 70 characters or less
- Summarize the page's value
- Contain keywords (but don't overdo it)

Inform, build your authority, and add a hook to get searchers to click. For example, if we were selling apples, here might be a sample title tag:

"The Ultimate Guide of Delicious Red and Green Organic Apples"

For social share-worthiness, you want these attributes:

- Emphasis on emotion is more important than keywords
- Title should be descriptive and include a call-to-action
- Shock or arouse curiosity

If you use the same example of selling apples but want to make it more appealing for social sharing, you might use a title closer to this:

"Are Organic Apples Really Healthy? Click to See 13 Reasons Red Apples Are Better Than Green."

Myth #6
A Link is a Link

When another website hyperlinks to your website, it may be indicative of your website's importance and popularity. Google may boost your rankings based on the quality and quantity of these backlinks. Emphasis should be given to the word "quality," not quantity. Due to Google's 2012 Penguin algorithm, long gone are the days of submitting or acquiring mass quantities of links from low-quality websites.

Google Penguin

From Wikipedia, the free encyclopedia

Google Penguin is a codename[1] for a Google algorithm update that was first announced on April 24, 2012. The update was aimed at decreasing search engine rankings of websites that violate Google's Webmaster Guidelines[2] by using now declared black-hat SEO techniques involved in increasing artificially the ranking of a webpage by manipulating the number of links pointing to the page. Such tactics are commonly described as link schemes.[3] According to Google's John Mueller,[1] Google has announced all updates to the Penguin filter to the public.[4]

What's a quality backlink then? One that is from a respected, non-spammy website that is relevant to your industry.

Myth #7
Low Domain Authority is Contagious

Domain Authority ("DA") is a metric created by Moz.com that, more or less, was intended to replace Google's former "PageRank" metric that assigned a quality value to a website.

https://en.wikipedia.org/wiki/PageRank

It sounds like something good to pay attention to, right? Sure, but some SEO companies spend *too* much time focusing on getting links from *only* high DA websites. While a high DA site is nice, it's not the only way. Think about it. Every site isn't going to be as high of a DA as Wikipedia. In the real world, most websites are just average.

Let's say you live in a small farming town and run a wedding venue. In this case, your industry is comprised of everyday sites that are mostly "low DA." In that case, it is then okay, if not equally valuable, to get links from other small town websites that talk about weddings, photography, etc.

Myth #8
"Link" is Just Another Word For Conversion

Not so. Links are like turning on the porch light, so that passers-by can see you. It's warm and inviting, but they aren't going to come up and knock just because you turned on the light.

More isn't always better, either. Stringing more and more lights all over your roof won't make a big difference, and neither will hoarding more untargeted backlinks. No one is going to click. Therefore, no one is going to convert.

If you have picked up on the repetitive theme here, quality links—not just lots of links—attract people to click on your site. Once they stop by for a visit, you must compliment your marketing efforts with compelling content and good user experience.

Myth #9
The More Outgoing Links, the Merrier

In general, outgoing links are not bad. In most cases, they are just neutral, but no ranking benefits should be expected purely based on outbound links.

However, some companies with outdated concepts of SEO best practices swap links between all of their clients' websites. Doing so dilutes the value of your real links. Additionally, if you begin to harbor enough mutually exchanged links, you create a pattern that Google may penalize you for, as they see this as attempting to manipulate search results based on artificial backlinks.

Myth #10
Slow and Steady Linking Wins the Day

The prevailing belief is that you will be penalized if you acquire too many backlinks too quickly. There is some truth to that, but it depends on the quality of the links being acquired.

Think of link building like running a marathon. You can run as fast as you like, but if you didn't stretch, it's going to hurt sooner than later. Instead, you have to improve the *quality* of your run by stretching first. Google's Penguin algorithm may penalize a site for going too fast, racing for low-quality links. However, if you acquire good backlinks, you have less to worry about. After all, sites that go viral don't get penalized after they get flooded with links.

Myth #11
Any Keyword Is As Good As The Next

To save time or money, many sites wander into the no man's land of unsearched keywords because they are easy targets. This is never a good tactic, because what's the point in being on page one of Google for a keyword that no one searches? Make sure that whatever words you target have enough search volume to justify your efforts. Do some competitive analysis and keyword volume research before starting your campaign.

Many online tools that can tell you approximately how many times a keyword is searched and how competitive it is to target, as well as suggesting other potentially related keywords to consider targeting.

1. **Google KeywordPlanner** - This is often the most recommended keyword research tool because the data comes directly from Google. To access this information, you will need a Google Ads account. You don't have to pay for an ad to go live, but you will need an ad account.

    https://ads.google.com/aw/keywordplanner/home

2. **trends.google.com** - Another free tool from Google that lets you compare the increases and decreases in how frequently a word or

phrase is searched. This will help you identify if the interest in a keyword has been increasing or decreasing over time.

3. **WordStream.com/keywords** - WordStream offers free and paid subscriptions to help you research keywords to target.

4. **WordTracker.com** - WordTracker provides insights into SEO and PPC data from Google, as well as data from their own search technology.

5. **AnswerThePublic.com** - This is probably my favorite resource for keyword research, content ideas, and creative thinking. You can use Answer the Public to input keyword ideas, and it will spit out examples of different ways that your customers are *already* searching Google for similar terms. Use these results to come up with an extensive list of keyword targets, keyword alternatives, and ideas for topics to build content around.

Myth #12
Rankings Are All That Matter

While rankings are one important metric, they do not ensure success. Rankings must convert to traffic, which must convert clicks to sales. Rankings are one part of a larger picture. User-experience is equally important because what good is all the traffic in the world if the users can't figure out how to complete a transaction? The combination of an effective marketing strategy and an intimate understanding of your customer's journey is where the real payoff occurs. SEO builds a road to your door, so make sure to leave it unlocked.

Myth #13
You Can Buy Your Way to the Top

Even though Google sells ads at the top of a page, the money spent on ads has no relation to showing up higher in the non-paid results. They're completely unrelated, so don't feel like you have to pour a lot of money into purchasing ads.

Myth #14
Invest a Penny to get A Million Dollars

We've all heard that if we doubled a penny every day for 30 days, we would have a million dollars. The only problem with that is there are very few places that will double your return like that. Where SEO is concerned, you get what you pay for. Better to live by the adage: it takes money (or time) to make money. Like a smart investment, SEO can yield huge returns as long as you're patient and invest in the right ways.

Myth #15
SEO Will Save Us!

SEO is powerful, but it is not a magical potion that can turn your business around in just a matter of days or even weeks. It is a strategy that requires advanced planning and time to work, and when a company is failing, it is too late to try SEO to save a sinking ship.

Chapter Nine

Size Matters

No matter where you dream of competing – locally, nationally, or globally – local SEO can be a profitable, less resistant point of entry. Given that there are thousands of new websites launching every day somewhere in the world, it is much easier to rank well in your local market than to take on a state, country, or the whole world. It's certainly possible to shoot for the moon, but it's easier to make progress locally and use that momentum to grow into larger markets.

But what is local SEO, and how does it differ from national SEO?

Local SEO is about driving website traffic, sales, and leads for a specific service to an equally specific location. An easy example would be a dentist in Salt Lake City, Utah.

National SEO is about driving that traffic on a national level. What this means, which is not so obvious, is that national SEO usually focuses more on your brand, not necessarily a specific location or service.

An example of using the momentum of local SEO to show up nationally is Starbucks. Each of their locations are highly optimized to show up for local searches. Therefore, that value is applied nationwide. Now, when anyone searches for "coffee near me," there is a good chance that Starbucks will show up anywhere, nationally.

In truth, not every business needs to make an effort to rank nationally. And even if national SEO does make sense, it may not be the best place to start on day one. If you have learned anything in this book so far it's that search intent matters. The goal of Google is to provide relevant information to a searcher. And local SEO might be your foot in the door.

It's simple math. Smaller location = less competitors = less search engine competition = easier to rank.

Additionally, targeting long-tail keywords in local search results converts higher. What do I mean by long-tail keywords? Here are two search query examples:

1. "Italian food"
2. "Italian restaurant with vegan options and wine."

The first search term could be from someone wanting to cook dinner themselves and looking for an Italian food market. But the second search term is very specific and would convert to a sale easier because it is clear that the searcher does not want a market and instead wants a restaurant

Extend your initial keyword research efforts to determine how your product is being searched locally (i.e., "where to buy 'your product/service' in 'your city'"). Don't be too dismayed if it is a small volume of searches, because they could be very targeted, implying high-value prospects.

There are four steps that you will want to undertake to get your site ready for local SEO.

1. Claim your Google My Business listing

Local SEO works best when you claim your Google My Business ("GMB") listing.

https://www.google.com/business/

Claiming your GMB page, and its Microsoft equivalent, Bing Places for Business, is vital for visibility in places like local maps results.

https://www.bingplaces.com

The catch? You must have a real and verified address. Google sends you a postcard with a code so you can verify that you're associated with the local address that you're claiming. PO boxes are not acceptable addresses, and, apparently other work-around options are losing validity as well, such as using the address of a UPS Store. If you try those sneaky alternatives, Google won't send you a postcard. No postcard, no Google-verified address.

If you have a small business or work out of your house and are willing to have clients or the public see your home address on Google maps, you can use your home address. However, I'd avoid that route for several reasons, not the least of which is your personal safety and what rapidly eroding shreds of privacy we still have left in our control today. Hopefully, you never have a disgruntled customer but, if you do, them showing up at your front door doesn't sound appealing.

2. Localize your website

Localizing your website means including your city, county, or region name naturally throughout your site. If you are a business that already operates with several locations, this could involve creating separate pages with unique content and value customized for those individual locations.

3. Get links and citations

Although I have warned you about directories being a lousy source of back-links, being featured on local sites, and moderated, quality-controlled business directories can sometimes be an exception. Emphasis on "moderated," "quality-controlled," and "sometimes."

4. Get reviews and ratings

Genuine, honest reviews are critical both for showcasing the quality of your service and for sending signals to search engines that your site and service are trusted and useful. The number of reviews you receive, the overall quality, the context of the reviews, and the authority of the review sites are all important factors for local search rankings. Getting the reviews is up to you. Whatever you do, take control. Otherwise, you will be fending off the disgruntled instead of attracting raving fans.

For more creative ways to acquire and leverage reviews to your benefit, see this article I contributed to for Forbes, titled "11 Authentic Methods Of Leveraging Customer Testimonials."

www.seonational.com/forbes-authentic-testimonials

"Setting expectations is key to customer satisfaction. But you can also set expectations to leverage reviews. Embrace sequenced emails or scheduled calls to let your customer know how far along into their journey with you they are. Let them know what you've accomplished and what's next. As you give these updates, ask them to share their positive experiences so far to score an authentic review."

One of the greatest parts about targeting local SEO first is that you're only trying to compete with companies nearby, as opposed to competing with everyone, everywhere. And let's not overlook that national brands have national sized budgets and marketing departments. Those are just a few of the many reasons that it makes sense to focus within your local area to grow a loyal customer base.

In this ever-expanding, borderless world we live in, there is no small amount of irony that it is local SEO that can allow a small upstart business to go toe-to-toe with mega-brands. It can be the saving grace of small businesses that are so vital to our economy.

Chapter Ten

25 Questions

W e live in the era of the fake guru. They are all over social media, with promises that they have hacked the code for overnight success if you adopt their simple system for a low price. Culturally, we seem to continue falling for these sales pitches as we desperately chase a quick fix to catapult us to the success we dream of.

Unfortunately, these fake gurus are not limited to one industry and SEO is full of them too. They prey on the under-informed with over-inflated promises of success and lowball pricing structures. They sound too good to be true – and they are, which brings us to where you probably are feeling stuck between a rock and a hard place.

Whether you are learning SEO for yourself or you don't want to get taken for a ride when hiring out your SEO, it's crucial to have a few questions answered that I outline in this chapter. I'll present the questions from the position of a customer. Likewise, if you offer SEO, your ability to answer these questions will build stronger relationships with your customers.

As a customer, choosing the right search engine optimization agency can be a challenging process. It is not unheard of for a business to run through a few SEO companies before they find the right one for them. That cycle can be time-consuming and costly.

The good news is that with the right questions, it's not that hard to sniff out if an SEO company is credible or a wolf in sheep's clothing. If you ask the following questions, you are well on your way to finding a partner who is likely to deliver what you need, and not take you for a ride.

Question #1
How long have you been doing this?

It makes sense to hire someone with at least a couple years of experience. Things can change from one Google update to the next, so look for somebody who takes a long-term approach rather than using techniques that might not work in a few months.

Question #2
Can you share past results?

Shopping for an SEO company is like most other things. You want to hear positive reviews and maybe testimonials or case studies of past customers. While you don't need to know their entire portfolio of clients, hopefully you'll recognize at least a handful of successful businesses on their roster.

If an SEO company can't provide you with a list of respectable clients, that's a red flag. Either they haven't helped any customers find success or they don't have experience at all.

Question #3
Who is your longest active client?

If you find a good tax accountant, you won't mind paying their fees because they'll save you enough in taxes to cover those costs. The same goes for good SEO. If an SEO company has been around for a few years but can't speak of any long-term clients, watch out. It makes no sense why any business would drop a consistently profitable source of revenue.

Need an example? Here is a retail client of mine and their traffic growth after one year of SEO.

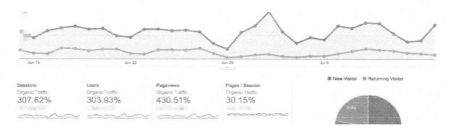

Then year two.

Year three.

Or the client, a marketing director, that messaged me that he was due for a raise thanks to his company being up $700,000+ in sales after their first quarter of search engine optimization.

Or this client that made over two million dollars in just three months.

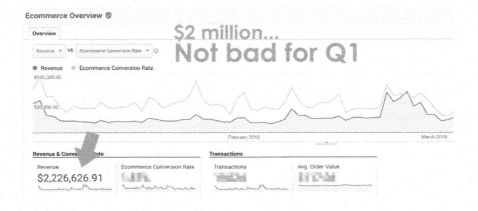

You can see why, with this type of return, a good SEO company should be able to keep clients long-term.

Question #4
What kind of clients do you typically work with?

It is possible to cast too wide of a net when asking this question, but it is also possible to be too narrow. As a point of clarification, an SEO company doesn't have to focus on a specific niche. Good SEO companies should have a proven process that they can roll out to any client in any industry.

On the other side of the coin, and more often than I wish I had to admit, I regularly see industry-specific "SEO companies" do more harm than good. Usually, when I see "dentist SEO" or "attorney SEO" companies, I cringe a little. I'm sure not all are bad, but most results that I see from these types of companies are full of website templates that are mass-produced with the same crap content duplicated on site after site after site. This leaves customers with a website that doesn't perform well and content that Google penalizes them for since it's not unique.

What is important is to find a company that has experience with the type of SEO <u>campaign</u> you'll need. An example of this is the difference between local and national SEO campaigns. If you're a local business, then you'll want to make sure that your SEO company is experienced with local SEO. If the SEO you need is for a national campaign, the SEO company should have experience in such a competitive space, because that's a different beast.

Question #5
How will you get to know my business?

Understanding a company is much more than just knowing industry terminology. For search engine optimization to be successful, an SEO company must truly understand the client's business, company goals, target demographics, the needs of those buyers, their habits, what questions they could benefit from being answered, their pain points, and more. Otherwise, the SEO company won't feed Google the relevant information that it needs.

It's also vital that you understand what marketing efforts are -or should be- driving your business. For example, one client that I worked with was a law firm that had previously worked with an internet marketing company that allocated 80 percent of its advertising budget to "workers' compensation law." However, workers' compensation only accounted for 15 percent of the law firm's revenue. If your SEO company doesn't understand which markets, services, and products are driving your revenue, your entire strategy can be misaligned.

I recommend every SEO company and their client talk before officially launching an SEO campaign. This allows the agency to get more familiar with their customer, their value propositions to leverage for SEO, and their customer's goals. It also allows the customer to better understand SEO and what level of involvement they're expected to participate. And you should participate.

Question #6
How will you improve my search engine rankings?

Modern SEO requires a holistic strategy and experienced execution, and if an agency is doing this right, they will be transparent about their strategy. But if an SEO company dances around explaining their processes, they probably aren't qualified or just want to cash your check and don't care about results.

All good SEO companies have a process. While there may be variations in the details of how they do their work, there will be little variation in the core principles that they touch on. They should describe how they balance three major components of SEO, considering each vital.

- on-page optimization
- content strategy
- off-page optimization (backlinks/citations)

1 - On-page optimization improves the efficiency of a website's structure, page speed, mobile-friendliness, and other technical aspects that could impact search engine traffic. If an audit of your website isn't part of an SEO company's processes, they likely aren't very good at search engine optimization. During a website's structure audit, an SEO professional will make sure that search engines can crawl the site, identify weaknesses contributing to poor page speed, fix SEO basics like title tags and meta descriptions, correct dead pages and broken links, and will analyze content, among other tasks.

2 - Content strategizing should include the creation and distribution of content both on the website and to third-party websites. The website's existing content should be reviewed to determine the most valuable pages, what existing pages could benefit by being elaborated within, and any gaps in keyword targets that need entirely new pages built out. There should also be a strategy mapped out to support on-going content creation as well as authoring content on third party sites for increased credibility and backlinks.

3 - Off-page optimization means improving your website's external credibility. This is done by strengthening your brand awareness, creating and distributing content about your product or service, and looking for opportunities to increase your domain and page authority by getting other high-quality, relevant websites to link to your website or talk about your company. It often makes sense to have your off-page optimization strategy overlap with your content strategy.

Effective SEO takes time, and there are no guarantees (I'll explain why in one of the upcoming questions), but that shouldn't prevent an experienced agency from giving you a high-level explanation of where they will start. Although it is unlikely that you will hear "We're going to get links from X, Y, and Z websites," what the company should be able to explain to you is something along the lines of, "We'll start with an on-site technical SEO audit to identify any areas for quick wins. Then, we'll focus on a content strategy that includes steps A, B, and C."

Question #7
Ask about backlinks

Backlinks — when another website links to yours — have been important to SEO since Google came onto the scene with their PageRank algorithm, and that's not going to change any time soon.

What is PageRank and why are backlinks valuable? PageRank is a core part of Google's algorithm that counts when other websites link to you as a "vote" in the search engine popularity contest. And because one good backlink is more valuable than multiple cheap alternatives, quality is more important than quantity.

No self-respecting SEO would pursue low-quality backlinks, and the shady ones won't admit to it, so it is up to you to get a feel for how an SEO provider might approach backlinks. While there are countless ways to pursue back-links, two methods to stay away from would include any mention of the words "forum signatures" (stuffing a link in a never-to-be-used-again forum bio) or "link directories" (websites that exist as worthless list of links, unused by real humans, just to get a link).

A good SEO company can and will communicate transparently about their link building strategies. So if anyone says they can't discuss their methods because "they're proprietary," run!

Question #8
Do you always follow Google's best practices?

You have to play nice with Google if you want Google to play nice with you. Otherwise, your website may perform a disappearing act from Google in the form of a search engine penalty. Your SEO should be able to give you an idea of how well they follow Google's recommended best practices, or at least be candid of where they may push the boundaries. Because if you push too hard, you crash hard.

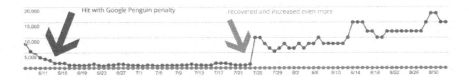

It can take months or even years of recovery work to correct a search engine penalty, and you'll be missing out on all of that revenue during this time. This is why safer, long-term SEO strategies are better than corner-cutting techniques.

At a minimum, you'll want someone who stays up to date with the information posted by Google on its Webmaster Central Blog, which is Google's outlet for news on how to best work within their search algorithms.

https://webmasters.googleblog.com

Better is someone who follows popular industry blogs and participates in SEO forums and conversations. The best SEO professionals will do all of the above as well as conduct their own research. They monitor websites that they manage for signs of impact from algorithm changes and investigate potential changes in SEO best practices.

Question #9
What do you need from me to be effective?

Legitimate SEO companies should respond with a long list of questions and needs. To conduct their work effectively, they'll need website logins, detailed information about your target audience, industry, goals, and Key Performance Indicators (KPIs), which are a set of measurable values that demonstrate the effectiveness of a marketing strategy. An experienced SEO company will need to work *with* their customer to be effective in working *for* them.

Effective SEO requires a partnership between multiple teams and company leaders, so agencies that need very little from you are unlikely to build an SEO plan that will help you achieve long-term success. But if you have done your homework, they will also be able to do theirs, and that's a beautiful thing.

Question #10
How will you keep me informed of website changes?

Once you have picked your SEO partner, the first thing you'll need to provide them with will be access to your website. Some people are paranoid about granting such access and try to mitigate risks by having changes that their SEO company suggests made by an in-house website developer. The obvious consequence is that changes will be made slower, less accurate, and you will have to make sure there is an open and constant line of communication between your developer and your SEO company, slowing your SEO campaign's overall progress. Are you willing to spend time being the middleman at the expense of delaying SEO progress? This is one of the main reasons it's important to hire an SEO company that you can trust.

A good SEO company will send you regular status updates. The most common frequency is once per month. Many will even offer to send reports more frequently at first, if you choose. Then, once all of the "heavy lifting" is done, changing to a quarterly reporting frequency is common.

Therefore, you should have great concern if an SEO consultant doesn't ask for any website changes to be made. If this happens, it's a *red flag*. While off-site work is a large part of SEO, it's only effective if your on-page optimization is solid first.

Question #11
How do you conduct keyword research?

In the past, keyword research meant plugging a term into a keyword research tool, populating a list of relevant keywords, and developing content with keywords inserted at various places. However, modern keyword research requires much more effort—it's an exercise in understanding the user's intent, search volume, and competitive landscape. There is an art to understanding what information a user is looking for when searching a keyword phrase, then providing content catered to the intent behind the search. This is particularly important based on you or your target audience's geographical location.

For example, if you search "oil" from a Las Vegas location, you get these results from Google's auto-suggest.

oil|

oil **change**
oil **change near me**
oil **prices**
oil
oil **change coupons**
oil **pulling**
oil **diffuser**
oil **of oregano**
oil **can harry's**
oil **filter**

If you search the same word from a Wyoming location, you get different suggestions.

oil|

oil **price**
oil
oil **pulling**
oil **rig**
oil **price chart** pons
oil **painting**
oil**ers**
oil **news**
oil**ily**
oil**atum**

It's not just the auto-suggested search terms that are different based on a searcher's location, but the actual search results are different, too. For example, here is a search for "real" in Texas.

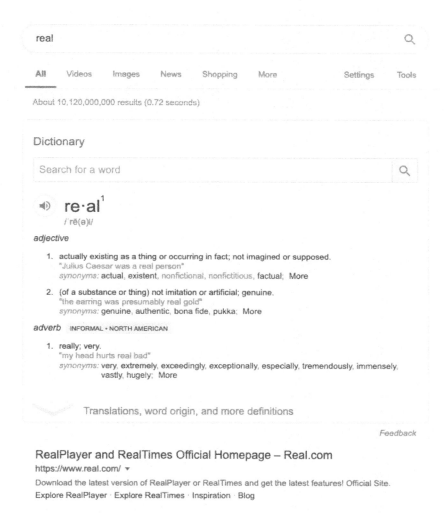

Here is the same search, but from a Utah location.

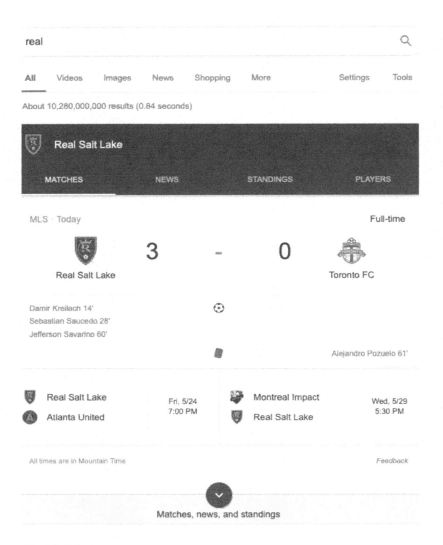

Real Salt Lake
https://www.rsl.com/ ▾
Zions Bank **Real** Academy. Now Enrolling for the 2018-19 School Year. Learn More ... **Real** Monarchs · **Real** Monarchs Season Tickets · Palma Named to ...
Schedule · Tickets · Players · Real Monarchs | Real Salt Lake

Real | Definition of Real by Merriam-Webster
https://www.merriam-webster.com/dictionary/real ▾
Real definition is - having objective independent existence. How to use **real** in a sentence. Synonym Discussion of **real**.

You can see that Google caters to the likelihood that searchers in Utah are looking for info on the local professional soccer team, Real Salt Lake.

As you're interviewing prospective SEO companies, make sure that they ask you about your geographical targets, and speak about the tools and methodologies they use to determine user intent. If the entire conversation revolves only around how many times a keyword is searched, whether applicable to your targets or not (like how Utah's Real soccer team is less relevant to anyone outside of Utah), and there is no discussion about user intent or customer demographics, they're likely using outdated practices, or they use a cookie-cutter approach for all of their customers, and they don't personalize SEO campaigns to your specific needs. After all, it's better that your SEO strategy produces 100 *targeted* visitors per day and converts at 3% than targeting too broadly and getting 500 visitors per day with no conversions.

Question #12
What tools do you use?

Knowing exactly what tools an SEO company uses isn't necessarily important, but knowing that they can describe *why* they use those tools is. Legitimate SEO professionals will have several tools they use to conduct audits and complete tasks, and they will have tested multiple tools to find the best. Ask the following questions:

- What tools do you use to conduct keyword research, and why?
- What website auditing tools do you use, and why?
- What do you use to conduct competitor analysis, and why?
- What do you use to monitor backlinks, and why?
- What do you use to monitor rankings, and why?

Your SEO partner should be able to articulate the reason their preferred tools are used and the impact those tools can have when properly utilized—not merely recite a long list of "great tools."

Question #13
What metrics do you track?

SEO can get technical, so you don't need to know everything, but most SEO companies will likely tell you that they track:

- **Rankings** – You should be able to keep tabs on what target keywords are moving up (or down) with ranking reports.
- **Traffic** – A traffic report should show your search traffic for a specific timeframe (i.e., a month or year) compared against a previous range.
- **Conversions** – Experienced SEO companies know that the money is in conversions. Without a conversion, there is no return on investment and any traffic increase is just a vanity metric.

While all three metrics are important, you can't track conversions without traffic, nor traffic without rankings. If your website is new, track rankings until you get some visibility on page one of Google. Page one will then bring traffic, which means you can then track that and conversions.

Question #14
How do you determine if you're successful?

To gauge the success of SEO, you must track how much traffic is coming into your website and where it is coming from. This can be done via Google Analytics.

https://analytics.google.com

However, as mentioned in the previous question, it is unlikely that you will get much traffic until your website shows up on page one of Google. Until then, you can track the improvements of how far back your website shows up in search results for your target keywords. Is your website improving from page ten to seven, then seven to four, then three, then two, and finally page one?

Once on page one, does your SEO company consider your campaign a success only once they get you to #1 on page one, in the top three, or is anywhere on page one sufficient? Because there is a big difference between the traffic that a number one position drives (about 33% of all clicks) versus the number ten spot (less than 5%), both of which are on page one.

While you're waiting on your website's journey towards page one, you can also keep a pulse on Google Search Console.

https://www.google.com/webmasters/tools/siteoverview

Is your SEO provider identifying, acknowledging, and fixing errors that Google reports? If so, you should see these "marked fixed" and reduce in quantity over time.

Be sure to ask how often they plan to share these important analytics with you and how they will use the data to improve your search engine rankings and website traffic continually.

You may have other key performance indicators that you have in mind. Transparency is key. The clearer you are on what you expect from your SEO provider, and the better they understand what those expectations are, the less frustration both of you will experience.

There are no right or wrong answers here, and if their expectations do not meet yours, then you can discuss what is reasonable. Whatever their response is, it will help you determine if you think a successful result on their end would justify the investment you're about to make on yours.

Personally, the more that I can educate my clients, the better. If I can help them understand the processes, then they'll be able to better support my efforts by feeding me what I need to then feed Google.

Question #15
Who does what work?

This question will help you know what to expect from whom at the SEO company, or even yourself, especially when it comes to content creation. For example, many SEO companies typically create content on your behalf, but not all of them do. You need to know what is expected from you and whether you have the bandwidth and skill to deliver content, if that is something that is expected of you.

If the SEO company creates content, ask for a copywriting sample to make sure that you're comfortable with the quality. You'll want to ensure that they have a process in place to close the knowledge gap of what you know about your industry versus what they need to know. The SEO company should be able to explain how they will educate themselves up to your level so that they can create accurate, optimized content that represents you properly.

Additionally, you want to make sure you're hiring the actual provider of the services, rather than hiring a firm who will subcontract the work out to another company. Some SEO companies charge high rates then outsource the work to low-quality freelancers. This leads to content that is full of errors or has a tone that doesn't properly connect with your audience.

Knowing your point of contact and having clear expectations from the start will maximize communication and minimize frustrations on both sides.

Question #16
Can you tell me about an unsuccessful campaign?

Most SEO companies have had missteps in the past. That's how you learn. Whether their fault or lack of participation from their client, it's great to hear why it didn't perform — and, more importantly, how they corrected for the future.

Question #17
Ask about algorithms

Most Google algorithm updates have a minor impact on any one site. However, some algorithms were significant enough to be named; Panda, Penguin, Hummingbird. Any qualified SEO should be familiar with the majority of these. If you'd like to familiarize yourself, Moz is a good resource.

https://moz.com/google-algorithm-change

Here are additional resources that keep track of algorithm changes.

- https://algoroo.com
- https://www.advancedwebranking.com/google-algorithm-changes/

It might feel a bit like entrapment, but you owe it to yourself to ask your potential SEO provider to describe a few algorithm updates, and then confirm that they know what they're talking about. It's not vital that they know the exact date of an update, but if they can say: "Google's most infamous algorithm updates, Panda and Penguin, rolled out around 2011 and 2012. But that was forever ago. More recently, there was X update, and then Y update a few months before that," that's a good sign that they likely know their stuff.

All you're trying to do here is filter out incredibly inexperienced SEOs or the ones that are just trying to make a quick buck without having much real-world expertise in the field.

Question #18
Have you worked with penalized sites?

Penalties weren't always part of the SEO landscape. But, primarily since those 2011 and 2012 algorithms I just mentioned, both manual and algorithmic penalties have skyrocketed. If your SEO has been working for at least a few years, they've no doubt been involved in working with a penalized site. Once a site has been hit with a penalty, it can be time-consuming to recover. However, good SEOs can still have a pretty high success rate.

Find out how successful your potential SEO company has been at bringing sites back from the brink, as well as how they will prevent those penalties from occurring in the future.

Question #19
How will we continue to communicate?

SEO is different from other services in that you don't typically need to contact your SEO company more than a few times a month. However, if something does go wrong, or you have an important issue to discuss, you want to be able to reach them quickly.

The communication styles and customer service standards of SEO companies will vary. Find out which methods of communication they prefer, and also tell them yours. You need to find someone whose approach best fits your needs. Ask if the candidate prefers to talk in person or via phone, Skype, text, or email. Find out how often they will reach out to you with status updates. Also, ask how to contact them in case of emergencies, which might include situations such as the site going down or search traffic dramatically declining.

Question #20
What's the cost?

Different SEO companies have different payment structures. It's important to know how much and when you will need to pay so that you can factor it into your budget.

Earlier, we discussed ROI and the importance of investing in long-term marketing strategies. This is where you will be required to find your investment tolerance. If the SEO company has a minimum of $2,000 per month and your budget is only $500 per month, then that's going to present a problem. Naturally, it's good to find that out sooner than later and to ensure your expectations are realistic within your budget.

Question #21
How long is the commitment?

It's important to know what you're getting yourself into. Understandably, most SEO's want you to sign on for a minimum time frame. Obviously, flexibility in terms is nice. However, long-term commitments aren't necessarily a bad thing with SEO.

Depending on the level of competition in your industry, it might require several months, even years, to generate results, and it's good for both the SEO company and you to be realistic about what it'll take. Knowing that SEO will take time, find the right balance between your level of patience and the reality of the scope of SEO work ahead.

Question #22
What happens if I terminate the contract?

As you know by now, SEO takes time. At the same time, if your business has a crisis and suddenly can't afford to pay for SEO services, you need to know your options. There might be other scenarios in which you would want to break the contract, too. Regardless, find out if there are any fees written into the contract for early termination.

Question #23
Are you working with any of my direct competitors?

An SEO company having multiple clients in the same industry is okay. The key question is, do they have the same keyword targets? Because there's only one spot at the top.

You should avoid a conflict-of-interest situation where an SEO company is having two of its clients compete head-to-head for the same keyword targets. It may seem self-evident, but if you don't ask, you may never know.

Question #24
Why should we hire you over other SEOs?

This is a very open-ended question. It doesn't have a right answer. Ideally, when you ask this question, your SEO provider will respond by pointing to their track record that should include successes from current and past clients, and they'll touch on the reputation they've built for themselves.

If they respond with any of the following, proceed cautiously.

- **We're cheaper than others** - Good SEO will not come cheap because good SEO is time intensive. It is an investment that can add tens or hundreds of thousands of dollars to your bottom line; potentially millions.
- **We can build you *more* backlinks** - Good SEOs will emphasize backlink quality, not quantity. Even if that means their link building strategy will take more time.
- **We can get faster results** - No good SEO would guarantee time frames. And if the SEO you're interviewing is advising you to cut corners, then it's best to move on to the next candidate - more on this in the next question.

Any good SEO company should also have a reference that they can provide you with. A more established SEO company should have several references available to you that can speak about the successes that were achieved working with them.

Don't forget to conduct a simple Google search of the SEO company's name to see if they rank in their local market. If not, ask why they don't practice what they preach?

Question #25
Can you *guarantee* number one rankings?

Anyone promising #1 rankings every time is not telling the truth. And if they go further and make that guarantee in a specific time frame, head for the hills. Although the myth persists that this is possible, here are the reasons that it is highly unlikely.

- **Google's algorithm remains a mystery to us all** - Google is in business to make money – lots and lots of money. Billions of dollars, to be specific. If anyone cracked Google's search engine algorithm, their revenue would be vulnerable. SEO companies can catch glimpses, read insights from Google's publications and patent filings, or conduct their own research to identify search engine opportunities, but Google isn't sharing otherwise.

- **Algorithm changes are constant** - Given that algorithms change daily, even if someone figured it out, it wouldn't be the same the next day. There are certainties we can count on, but the changes are frequent enough to undermine any guarantees of success in a given window of time.

- **Risky business** - Driving 20 mph over the speed limit might not get you into trouble if you don't get caught. However, the consequences can be substantial if you do. Likewise, Google regularly rolls out manual and algorithmic speed traps. Trying to expedite your rankings with shortcuts may seem harmless at first, but the chances of you eventually getting caught are high and the aftermath makes it a game that you don't want to play.

Good SEO Is A Two-way Street

A successful relationship with an SEO company is a partnership built on mutual understandings. You're both pursuing the same goal—to increase your revenue. Work together from the start and decide how you can assist each other in reaching those goals.

Some clients may complain that they have to play an active role in SEO with their agency of choice. While this is understandable, no one knows your business better than you. Use your industry expertise and what you've learned about SEO in this book to help your SEO company help you. By working together, you can learn to capitalize on each other's strengths. And when you take ownership of your SEO goals and spend time finding the right SEO partner, you are guaranteed to find success quicker.

Chapter Eleven

The Future of SEO

Technology is growing at an exponential pace. It is increasingly easy to underestimate what trend is rushing towards us at this very moment. I'm not talking only about SEO – I'm talking about every type of technology possible – from commerce to communications, to medical nano-technology, to smart homes and alternate, virtual realities.

Nothing – absolutely nothing – will be immune to this tech tidal wave. It is transforming so rapidly, in fact, that it has outstripped our ability to predict it.

According to The Emerging Future, in the next decade, technology will be 1,024 times more advanced than today, and 1,048,576 times more advanced in the decade that follows that. They also predict that in the next twenty years it will have become over a million times more advanced.

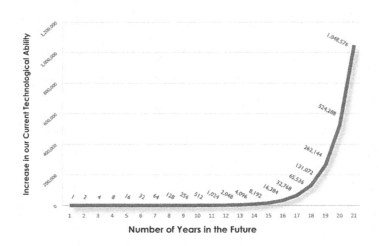

http://theemergingfuture.com/speed-
technological-advancement-charts.htm

Whether they are 100% accurate in their predictions is not as critical as the trend that they are identifying.

SEO will morph right along with this broader technological transformation. Consumer buying will follow where the technology leads, and SEO is all about finding your customers at the precise moment they are trying to find you. Google's algorithm, which is a reliable indicator of how other search engines will follow, has hundreds of factors that must be incorporated into your SEO strategy. This makes it a complex animal already that is likely to become even more complicated as new trends and technologies are introduced.

So this is the point where I get to go out on a limb and make a few predictions. Anyone who predicts the future is likely to become further off track the further out they attempt to predict. Still, the horizon is already showing enough interesting trends worth mentioning that we don't have to guess too wildly.

It isn't about knowing what the new factors will be, because those will rapidly evolve as technology does. It's about becoming a student of human nature and monitoring the impact of trends as they happen so that you can evolve your marketing strategies with the opportunities that present themselves. That is just one more reason you will ultimately want an SEO expert on your team because SEO is going to get even more complex and interesting, very fast.

Here are ten examples of how search engines -and SEO- are transforming.

1. The Rise of the Visual; Video and Images

Increasingly, it's getting harder to trick Google into thinking that you have great content if you really don't. Especially when content is becoming increasingly visual, and search engines are already giving those visual assets greater emphasis. From photos to infographics, and most noticeably video, the shift from text to imagery is not going to diminish any time soon.

This change in content has been the result of quicker internet speeds and social media grooming us to consume more visual content. As a result, Google and other search engines are already embracing fresh, unique images and videos, giving them greater prominence than before.

2. Is Anybody Listening?

You bet search engines are listening – to the sound of your voice. They are listening more intently and accurately than ever before.

Creepy? Maybe a little.

- https://www.bloomberg.com/news/articles/2019-04-10/ is-anyone-listening-to-you-on-alexa-a-global-team-reviews-audio
- https://www.washingtonpost.com/technology/2019/05/06/ alexa-has-been-eavesdropping-you-this-whole-time/

Profound? Unquestionably.

Voice search will continue to increase rapidly alongside the rise of smartphones and smart speaker sales like Amazon Echo and Google Home. Google reports nearly half of adults and more than half of teens use voice search daily.

https://www.mobilemarketer.com/ex/mobilemarketer/ cms/news/search/18923.html

Further, Google's Behshad Behzadi says that voice search usage is growing faster than regular typed in searches.

https://www.bruceclay.com/blog/keynote-the-future-of-search-smx/

That opens up a whole new world of keyword search considerations for SEO. For example, when you type in a question we've been trained to type using broken sentences to, hopefully, return more accurate search results. But voice searchers ask questions like they would in any other conversation, except they ask it to a search engine. Because voice searches are activated by voice and provide spoken search results, users are starting to favor vocally initiated search engine results because of their intuitiveness. Over time, this will drastically alter the format of searches and, of course, search engine results.

The important thing to understand about voice search (as well as every other trend in this chapter) is that as search engines evolve, the real change is usually in how search engines output results to users. The input – which is what your website feeds to the search engines – is still primarily influenced by regular optimization tactics and efforts; good content, fast page load, mobile-friendly design, etc.

3. Be Smart About Mobile

You cannot afford to ignore mobile SEO. In fact, mobile use is driving most of the changes we are seeing in SEO today. More than half of all searches on Google now come from mobile devices, and depending on your specific industry, mobile searches may drive as much as 90% of your traffic. This makes mobile-friendliness a factor for ranking that will continue to increase in importance.

Where Google once gave priority to desktop sites, mobile pages now receive greater priority. This is what is being referred to as "mobile-first" – the prioritization of mobile-friendly websites.

Google has taken it upon itself to encourage the web to become a more mobile-friendly place and has been rewarding sites that offer mobile compatibility with higher rankings. Search engines want users to be able to quickly load your website's content on their phone, read the text without having to zoom or scroll horizontally, and easily push any links and buttons.

In today's hectic world, it's also worth noting that when something comes to a customer's mind that they take action on their mobile device in micro-moments. As a business, you must consider these micro-moments that last mere seconds. This translates into a simple but enormous shift for companies to focus on mobile-friendliness. Your website navigation must be intuitive, contact information should be visible, and phone numbers should be clickable for one-touch dialing. When your website loads "correctly" like this, you will be rewarded with higher rankings.

Google has set the pace for the future of mobile searches and is broadcasting its intent to anyone who is listening. This is apparent, as Google has been steadily rolling out new features that favor mobile-exclusive functionality for years, and this trend will continue.

4. Survival of the Fastest

Speed is a prerequisite for almost everything in our lives today. Fast-food, fast-growth, speed-dating, instant results, immediate feedback – and yes, instant search results. In today's fast-paced, on-demand society, people want things, including information, immediately.

You know the frustration of visiting a website, only to have to wait for what seems like an eternity for the page to load? That "eternity" is probably closer to 5 seconds.

Good page speed is a user experience feature that is expected of all websites, and search engines are paying close attention. You don't like slow websites, and neither do your customers, so Google doesn't either. If your website is slow, your rankings will suffer, which means less traffic and sales. Speed as a ranking factor is only going to increase.

If you're wondering how fast is fast enough, most in the industry will tell you the goal is three seconds or less. To see how the speed of your website stacks up, you can test it with Google's PageSpeed Insights.

https://developers.google.com/speed/pagespeed/insights/

Or an alternate, and my favorite, GTmetrix.com.

5. Increasingly Personalized Results

Google, Bing, and Yahoo all personalize their search results in multiple ways, and personalized search results aren't just based on traditional ranking factors but also on the information about the user, such as their location, search history, and identifiable interests.

https://www.link-assistant.com/news/ranking-factors.html

Google has been pushing more personalized search results, especially since they introduced Gmail in 2004. Since then, any time that you login to a Google platform with your Gmail login, they can catalog a user's search queries, allowing them to increase the accuracy of search results later. Additionally, with new advancements in technology on a seemingly daily basis, the growing popularity of smart speakers and personal assistant devices (Alexa, Siri, Google Assistant, Cortana, etc.), and the ability for big brother to log those voice searches like they do Gmail, personalized search results will likely increase even further in years to come.

6. Machine Learning May End Traditional Search Algorithm Updates

Google has invested heavily in machine learning and AI over the years. Eventually, we may see formal algorithm updates fade away entirely, in favor of dynamic and continuous algorithm changes carried out by machine learning. An example is Google's RankBrain project, which is their deepest dive into machine learning, interpreting search queries to influence search results.

- https://en.wikipedia.org/wiki/RankBrain
- https://searchengineland.com/
  faq-all-about-the-new-google-rankbrain-algorithm-234440

7. Expanding Search Engine Features

Increasingly, search engine features like local featured snippets and Knowledge Graph results are catching searchers' attention and stealing clicks away from what otherwise would have been an organic link to a website.

How so? These types of search results provide answers to a searcher's questions right on the screen.

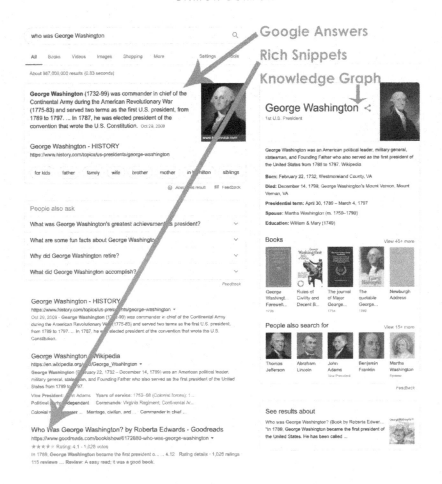

Google has been steadily increasing the usefulness and frequency of these featured snippets as the search engine aims to be the one-stop-answer-shop, eliminating the necessity for searchers to click through to a website to find their final answer.

who was the first president   🔍

All   Books   Images   Shopping   News   More   Settings   Tools

About 2,470,000,000 results (0.63 seconds)

President of the United States (1)

This immediate answer:
George Washington ⟵⟶
is stealing traffiic from
these organic results

People also search for   View 15+ more

Thomas Jefferson	Abraham Lincoln	John Adams	Benjamin Frankl	Martha Washington	James Madison	Theodore Roosevelt
		Vice President		Spouse		

Books and overview

Feedback

Articles of Confederation, US Constitution, Constitution Day Materials ...
https://www.constitutionfacts.com/us-articles-of-confederation/john-hanson-story/ ▾
In November 1781, John Hanson became the first President of the United States in Congress Assembled, under the Articles of Confederation. Many people have argued that John Hanson, and not George Washington, was the first President of the United States, but this is not quite true.

The First 10 Presidents of the United States and What They ...
https://www.history.com/news/first-10-us-presidents ▾
Feb 4, 2019 - On February 4, 1789, electors chose George Washington to be the first president of the United States. Washington's term, and those of the next ...

According to Perficient Digital, the trend of increased "rich answers" is only going to continue rising, having more than doubled from 2018-2019.

Total Rich Answers

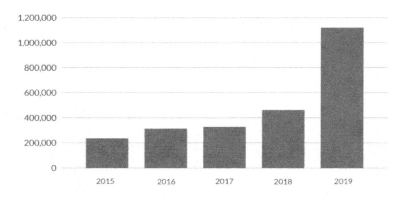

https://searchengineland.com/rich-answers-in-google-mobile-
search-more-than-doubled-since-2018-study-finds-325444

With the evolution of these expanded search results, it's critical that you:

- track your rankings within these features (in addition to your rankings within traditional organic search results), and
- monitor which snippet formats show up for your keywords and are potentially stealing traffic from you.

While there are several tracking solutions available, two that I use are:

I. SEO PowerSuite's Rank Tracker and
    www.seonational.com/rankings

II. Advanced Web Ranking
    www.seonational.com/tracker

Both can track where your website ranks. Not only in the traditional ten organic positions per page, but also within snippets, maps, image results, and more.

But with Google stealing these organic clicks, what are you to do? If you can't beat 'em, join 'em. If someone's website is going to be "the answer" that Google shows in a search result, why not have it be yours? At least that way you have a fighting chance to be clicked on.

A good place to start learning how to incorporate the unique code required to get your website recognized in these types of search results is Schema. org.

While embracing schema is not a tactic for a novice SEO, it does significantly increase your chances of showing up in search results in more unique, eye-catching ways. Who doesn't want five stars next to their website?

This increases your visibility, which increases clicks, which increases sales.

8. Relevance, Relevance, Relevance is the new "Location, Location, Location"

There are many ways Google analyzes the quality of a website's content. One way is by looking at billions of pages and verbiage used in them to learn which words are relevant to other variations in a certain context. This helps Google understand when words could be used interchangeably.

For example, if you are an attorney that has a lot of great information on your website and you rank really well for the phrase "injury attorney" but your site never uses the word "lawyer," there is still a strong chance that Google will use "attorney" and "lawyer" interchangeably and rank you for one if the other already ranks well.

With RankBrain, Google compares search results that performed well and looks for common factors to consider when displaying future search results.

> https://www.link-assistant.com/news/
> optimizing-for-semantic-search.html

In a way, the algorithm learns from itself based on how previous search results performed.

What can you do to make sure that your content is comprehensive? For starters, research the top-ranking pages in your niche and look for common characteristics that they share, just like RankBrain does. For example:

- what words are repeated on the page and how frequently
- how many words total are on the page
- and more examples in the next paragraphs

Doing this manually would be massively time-consuming. Fortunately, there is a report that already exists that can help you out. It's called TF-IDF, and it's available using one of my favorite platforms, SEO PowerSuite's WebSiteAuditor.

seonational.com/audit

Content Optimization: Summary

Title		Body	
Keywords in title	0	Keywords in body	2
Title length	31 chars	Word count in body	1,378
Multiple <title> tags	No	Keywords in H1	2
Meta tags		Keywords in H2-H6	0
Keywords in meta description tag	0	Keywords in bold	0
Meta description length	174 chars	Keywords in italic	0
Multiple meta description tags	No	Keywords in link anchors	0
Keywords in meta keywords tag	0	**Images**	
		Keywords in alt texts	0
		Empty alt texts	0

What is TF-IDF?

According to WebSite Auditor's website, "TF-IDF ('term frequency-inverse document frequency') is used to measure the importance of a given keyword on a page. Unlike keyword density, it doesn't just look at the number of times the term is used on the page; it also analyzes a larger set of pages and tries to determine how important this or that keyword is."

In short, it's not just how many times a keyword is mentioned within a page that ranks, but also how long their overall content is on that page, how many total characters, how many total words, how many times a target word shows in a title tag, in a meta description, etc.

In WebSite Auditor, jump to Content Analysis > TF-IDF and select a page. The program will go to Google's search results and analyze the ten top-ranking websites for the keyword(s) that you want to target. It will then calculate a TF-IDF score of keywords that show up in title tags, meta descriptions, image alts, and the content body. Afterward, you can consider editing your website to meet or exceed what your competitors are doing.

9. Links Without Links?

Since Google rolled on to the scene, acquiring links have been one of the biggest strategies used in optimizing a website. But search engines know that links are being abused, as eventually happens to most things in marketing. And so, as search engines look for additional positive ranking signals to consider, unlinked brand name or website mentions ("citations") are becoming an SEO strategy worth investing in. It's as simple as it sounds. Citations are when your company name or domain name is mentioned on another website but is not hyperlinked. Need more convincing?

- A patent by Google discusses "implied links." http://patft.uspto.gov/netacgi/nph-Parser?Sect1=PTO2&Sect2=HITOFF&p=1&u=%2Fnetahtml%2FPTO%2Fsearch-adv.htm&r=1&f=G&l=50&d=PALL&S1=08682892&OS=PN/08682892&RS=PN/08682892

- Gary Illyes, an analyst at Google, mentioned this concept in a keynote he presented. https://searchenginewatch.com/2017/09/27/the-last-word-on-fred-from-googles-gary-illyes/

- Duane Forrester, a former manager at Bing, confirmed that Bing is already using citations as a ranking signal. https://www.link-assistant.com/news/smx-west-2016-recap.html

10. SEO will expand beyond Google and Bing

Over the past few years, I've seen an increasing interest in optimizing for search engines outside of just Google. Google still dominates, remaining the most popular search engine by far. Yet, third-parties like DuckDuckGo for privacy, Amazon for retail, Facebook for social, and Yelp for local needs have stepped in to become relevant search engines in their own right. If you want to be found by a greater percentage of user searches, and introduce yourself to the broadest audience possible, you'll need to begin to think beyond Google's range of influence.

While there are shortcuts to get temporary gains on Google, gimmicks, and loopholes usually get abused by the SEO masses and eventually do more harm than good. If you avoid the shortcuts and stick to tried and proven methods, then you don't have to worry so much about what changes are lurking in the future. You have to decide if you are in it for a short-term money run or the long-term jackpot.

The best balance of speed, content, mobile-friendliness, and links will stand tallest. A gap in just one of those variables can make or break your ability to show up on search engines. And, be forewarned, the closer you want to get to the top of page one, the more these factors are going to matter, so pay attention to them from the beginning. After all, the top is where you want to be since as much as two-thirds of all clicks go to the first three search results.

Chapter Twelve

SEO Cheat Sheet

You now have all of the knowledge that is needed to show up higher on search engines and take your website to the next level. What I've taught you works with websites big or small. Adjust as needed based on your goals, time, and budget.

Let's now put your knowledge to use and map out your entire SEO strategy using what you've learned. I'll also throw in a few more last-minute secrets. Here we go!

To recap, search engines primarily look at three characteristics of your website.

1. How well it is built.
2. How good the content is.
3. How good of external credibility you have (backlinks, mentions, etc.)

How well your website is built

Does your website load quickly? Google basically says, "treat us like you treat a visitor." Since visitors don't like slow websites, neither does Google. Identify what is slowing down your site and fix it.

Use tools like Google PageSpeed Insights or GTmetrix to test your page speed. Three seconds or less is a home run.

- https://developers.google.com/speed/pagespeed/insights/

- https://gtmetrix.com

We live in a mobile world. Is your website mobile-friendly?

As of 2016, *most* websites had half of their traffic coming from people using mobile devices like phones or tablets than desktops or laptops. And, from my own experience, depending on your industry, some websites receive *more than 90%* of their traffic from mobile users.

Use Google's Mobile-Friendly Test to see how mobile-friendly your website is and how you can improve it.

https://search.google.com/test/mobile-friendly

Don't forget to clean up your SEO basics, too:

- broken links
- dead pages
- title tags
- meta descriptions
- heading tags

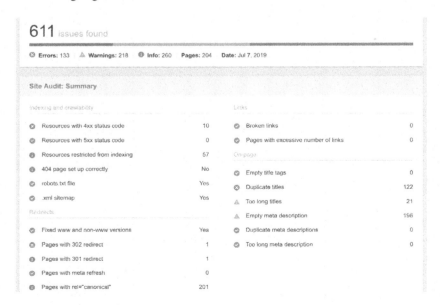

611 issues found

| ⊗ Errors: 133 | ⚠ Warnings: 218 | ⓘ Info: 260 | **Pages:** 204 | **Date:** Jul 7, 2019 |

Site Audit: Summary

Indexing and crawlability		Links	
Resources with 4xx status code	10	Broken links	0
Resources with 5xx status code	0	Pages with excessive number of links	0
Resources restricted from indexing	57	On-page	
404 page set up correctly	No	Empty title tags	0
robots.txt file	Yes	Duplicate titles	122
.xml sitemap	Yes	Too long titles	21
Redirects		Empty meta description	196
Fixed www and non-www versions	Yes	Duplicate meta descriptions	0
Pages with 302 redirect	1	Too long meta description	0
Pages with 301 redirect	1		
Pages with meta refresh	0		
Pages with rel="canonical"	201		

While variables like title tags and meta descriptions don't carry as much SEO weight as they used to, they should still be standard practice to optimize. Use a tool like Website Auditor to identify which of these variables could be improved.

www.seonational.com/audit

Now that your website's structure is dialed in, it's time to improve the content within it.

How good is your website's content?

Think about it. Google can only rank you for what it can read. If you have no content, how can Google identify what you offer and rank you for it? Or, if your content isn't unique, why would Google rank you uniquely?

Before you start producing content, you should know what keywords you want to target so that your content can support those targets. An excellent place to start is to search current trending topics and tie into what people are talking about so you can have immediate relevancy.

- Follow trending hashtags on Twitter
  - twitter.com/search-home
- Check what's trending on Google
  - trends.google.com/trends/
- See what BuzzSumo has to suggest for your industry
  - www.seonational.com/buzz
- Use my free recurring content ideas spreadsheet
  - www.seonational.com/free-seo-templates/

JANUARY TOPIC CONSIDERATIONS

HOLIDAYS & OBSERVANCES			
Date	**Holiday Name**	**Type**	**Where Observed**
Jan 01	New Year	Federal Holiday	Nationally
Jan 17	Benjamin Franklin's Birthday	Observance	Varies
Jan 20 (every 4 years)	Inauguration Day	State Holiday	Varies
Third Monday	Martin Luther King Day	Federal Holiday	Nationally
TOPICS			
Popular New Years Resolution	Drink Less Alcohol		
	Eat Healthy Food		
	Get a Better Education		
	Get a Better Job		
	Get Fit		
	Lose Weight		
	Manage Debt		
	Manage Stress		
	Quit Smoking		
	Reduce, Reuse, and Recycle		
	Save Money		
	Take a Trip		
	Volunteer to Help Others		
EVENTS			
Date	**Event**		
Jan 24	Belly Laugh Day		
Varies	Elvis Presley Birthday Celebrations		
Entire Month	Birth Defects Prevention Month		
	Cervical Health Awareness Month		
	Human Trafficking Awareness		
	National Blood Donor Month		
	National Mentoring Month		
	National Thank You Month		
	Thyroid Awareness Month		
FACTS			
Astrological Signs	Capricorn: December 22 - January 20 Aquarius: January 21 - February 19		
Birthstone	garnet		
Birth Flower	Carnation		

Another resource for content ideas is AnswerThePublic.com. Type in a keyword that you want to target or write about.

Answer The Public will kick out examples of different ways that your customers are *already* searching Google for variations of that word. Write content to answer those questions that are already being asked.

Here is an example of inputting "shoes" as a target keyword into Answer The Public. It comes back with this tree of questions that the public is already asking related to that keyword.

- can shoes be recycled
- can shoes be stretched
- how are shoes made
- can shoes shrink
- what shoes to wear with mom jeans
- why do shoes smell bad
- when is it okay to wear shoes without socks
- and on, and on, and on...

Write about that.

You can also use websites like SpyFu to identify what keywords your competitors are targeting.

www.seonational.com/spy

Type in a competitor's domain into SpyFu and scroll down to see some keywords that they're ranking for organically or that they're throwing a paid ad budget towards.

Top Keywords

Rank	Organic Keywords	SEO Clicks Per Month	Paid Keywords	Cost Per Click	Monthly Cost
1	shoe	200k	men's wide width shoes	$4.03	$1.25k

Chances are if they're throwing money at those keyword targets, it's because it is driving a return for them.

Another good strategy is to view the anchor text within your competitors' backlinks. Anchor text is the words that are linked within a hyperlink. For example, if I have a sentence that reads, "This is a great website, click to learn about shoes." And "click to learn about shoes" is linked, then that is the anchor text.

One of the SEO industry's favorite cloud-based backlink analysis tools is ahrefs.com.

My preferred desktop-based tool for reviewing backlinks is SEOspyglass.

www.seonational.com/backlinks

If you're looking for a free option, check out OpenLink Profiler.

www.seonational.com/olp

After you've identified the anchor text of your competitor, see if any of the keywords that they're targeting are worth considering targeting yourself.

Anchor text ❓	Uniques ❓
zappos	4,910
shoes	144
boots	72
sandals	45
sam edelman	42
converse	33
steve madden	32

We can't forget everyone's go-to keyword research tool, Google's Keyword Planner.

https://ads.google.com/aw/keywordplanner/home

An Adwords account is required to use the link above, but you are not required to spend money with it. Create an account and skip through the setup pages until you're able to come back and access Google's Keyword Planner.

Once you can access the Keyword Planner, continue by inputting a keyword. You'll get back a page of keyword targets to consider, as well as their historical search volume so you can identify which ones have the most potential.

Don't forget to also search your keyword considerations directly on Google. com to get an idea for how many competing results (other websites) you'll be fighting against for top rankings.

Once you have your list of keyword targets narrowed down, log them in a spreadsheet. You can download a free copy of the template that I use at www.seonational.com/free-seo-templates/.

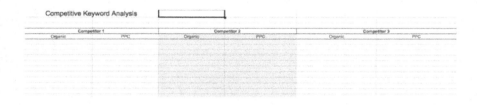

On that same link, you can also download a template to strategize a content calendar. That way, you can map out a 52-week content calendar, so when you find yourself in a good writing mood, you can hit the ground running and crank out a lot of good content instead of struggling over what to write about.

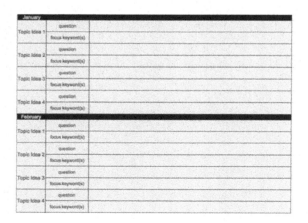

When the pen finally hits the paper, consider Grammarly. Grammarly helps keep your content, spelling, and grammar properly structured.

www.seonational.com/grammarly

While Grammarly focuses on spelling and grammar, Hemmingway focuses on readability.

If you are not a natural writer or if you need help scaling your content strategy, consider hiring a virtual assistant or outsourced copywriter. Here are two options:

1. Iwriter - www.seonational.com/writers

2. Fiverr - www.seonational.com/fiverr

While virtual assistants can be a great help, I'd only recommend bringing one on board *after* you've already approved your content calendar. That way, your writer will understand your keyword targets, overall goals, and will ensure that content stays on the right path.

Backlinks & External Credibility

Does your website have external credibility, like backlinks? A backlink is when another site links to yours. Backlinks are the metric that allowed Google to provide more accurate results than other search engines, even when they were the new kid on the block.

PageRank

From Wikipedia, the free encyclopedia
  (Redirected from Pagerank)

  "Google search algorithm" redirects here. For other search algorithms used by Google, see Google Penguin, Google Panda, and Google Hummingbird.

PageRank (PR) is an algorithm used by Google Search to rank web pages in their search engine results. PageRank was named after Larry Page,[1] one of the founders of Google. PageRank is a way of measuring the importance of website pages. According to Google:

  PageRank works by counting the number and quality of links to a page to determine a rough estimate of how important the website is. The underlying assumption is that more important websites are likely to receive more links from other websites.[2]

When other websites talk about you or link to your site, those actions act as a vote in a search engine popularity contest. The more links you have from relevant websites, the more that contributes to increased search engine rankings.

If you're in a local and non-competitive industry, you might be able to get away with more basic backlinks like blog commenting. Use a website like DropMyLink.com to identify potential sites to submit/ask/ acquire backlinks.

But, most sites require higher quality backlinks than that. In that case, a good strategy to start with is called "outreach," the process of reaching out to relevant websites or industry influencers and asking them to share or link to your content.

For outreach, use tools like BuzzSumo, Pitchbox, or NinjaOutreach.

- BuzzSumo - www.seonational.com/buzz
- Pitchbox - www.seonational.com/pitchbox
- NinjaOutreach - www.seonational.com/ninja

These tools will help you identify websites that are relevant to your niche, the types of content that perform well on their website (hint - write about those topics), and the contact information of the website owner or editors. Once you've identified good content to write about and share with these websites, reach out to the contacts that you found using the tools and build a relationship with those people to encourage engagement.

Congratulations

Google wants to show off websites that are an "authority" in their industry and that offer information that will best satisfy the searcher. Congratulations, you now have all of the strategies and tools that you need to be the authority.

Thank You

The most valuable commodity we have is attention, and our greatest asset is time. I'm humbled that you've given me your attention to share my experiences with you, and grateful for you sharing your time. Thank you for reading *Outrank*.

—Damon Burton

Keep your SEO-learning mommentum going and join Burton's free SEO Facebook group by visiting www.SEOnational.com/facebook.

Want to save time and hire Damon's team to do the work for you? Visit www.SEOnational.com.

Overview of Outrank

If you are ready to grow your online presence, Outrank is the place to start. Damon Burton, decades-long search engine optimization ("SEO") expert that's been featured by Forbes, Entrepreneur, and countless other media outlets, is the voice of reason, pulling back the curtain and showing readers detailed steps to outrank their competition.

Unphased by an increasingly noisy internet, Outrank takes no prisoners as it tackles the numerous myths and misconceptions about SEO and gives you a clear outline for increasing your visibility and profitability with search engines.

Given the rapidly changing search engine algorithms, Outrank boldly predicts trends that will impact online visibility into the next 5-10 years, putting readers ahead of the curve.

Although Outrank is a precise blueprint for increasing your online traffic, it also provides insights to make informed decisions about hiring and leveraging the right SEO company at the right time, should you prefer to hire an SEO expert instead of becoming one. Regardless of your business or budget, it is in reach to outrank your competition with Outrank.